THE BERND DEPARTMENT
OF ARCHITECTURE.

D1211644

WITHDRAWN
FROM THE COLLECTION
CARNEGIE LIBRARY OF PITTSBURGH

CLP-Main

APR 23 2003

Carnegie
Library of
Pittsburgh

Music and
Art Department

WITHDRAWN
FROM THE COLLECTION

UNIVERSITY BUILDERS

MARTIN PEARCE

UNIVERSITY BUILDERS

MARTIN PEARCE

q NA6600.P38 2001
Pearce, Martin.
University builders
Chichester : Wiley-Academy,
2001.

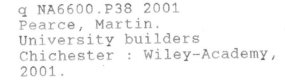

Photographic credits

Every effort has been made to locate sources and credit material but in the very few cases where this has not been possible our apologies are extended. All plans and drawings are courtesy of the architects. All photographs are courtesy of the architects unless otherwise stated: Martine Hamilton-Knight (courtesy of Michael Hopkins and Partners) pps 2, 126, 128–131; Soprintendenza Archeologica delle Province di Napoli e Caserta pg 17; Peter Cook/View pps 18, 21–23, 24, 27–29, 39–41, 42, 45–47, 96, 99–101, 114, 117–19, 164, 167–69, 188, 191, 193; Philippe Dureuil pps 30, 34–35; Davison & Associates Ltd pg 36; Sean Cooke pps 48, 51; Georges Fessy pps 52, 55–57; Dennis Gilber/View pps 64, 67–69, 79, 81, 85, 90–91, 120, 123–25, 132, 135, 137; James Morris/Axiom pps 70, 73–75; Paul Raftery pps 76, 80; Nigel Young/ Foster and Partners pg 82; John Edward Linden pps 86, 89, Matthew Weinreb pps 102, 105; Chris Mortimer (courtesy of Hampshire County Architects/Perkins Ogden Architects) pg 107; Kevin Purdy (© University of Portsmouth) pps 108 110–3; Christian Richters pps 138, 141–43, 145, 146; Daria Scagliola/Stijn Brakkee pps 149–51, Timothy Hursley pps 170, 173–76, 179–81, Katsuhisa Kida pps 182, 185–87, Richard Bryant/Arcaid pps 200, 203, 205, 207–10, 213–17

Cover: University of Portsmouth, Portland Street Building, Hampshire County Architects (photo: Kevin Purdy, © University of Portsmouth). Design by Artmedia Press, London
Frontispiece: Atrium of the University of Nottingham Jubilee Campus,
Michael Hopkins and Partners (photo Martine Hamilton-Knight)

First published in Great Britain in 2001 by
WILEY-ACADEMY

A division of
JOHN WILEY & SONS
Baffins Lane
Chichester
West Sussex PO19 1UD

ISBN: 0-471-988-340

Copyright © 2001 John Wiley & Sons Ltd. *All rights reserved.*
No part of this publication may be reproduced, stored in a retrieval system, or transmitted, in any form or by any means, electronic, mechanical, photocopying, recording, scanning or otherwise, except under the terms of the Copyright Designs and Patents Act 1988 or under the terms of a licence issued by the Copyright Licensing Agency, 90 Tottenham Court Road, London, UK, W1P 9HE, with the permission in writing of the publisher.

Other Wiley Editorial Offices
New York • Weinham • Brisbane • Singapore • Toronto

Set by BookEns Ltd, Royston, Hertfordshire
Printed and bound in Italy

CONTENTS

INTRODUCTION

Devoted to university builders, this title appears in the Wiley-Academy 'Builders' series, following those on, among others, church, museum, library and airport architecture. The following case studies provide an overview of a broad section of building for an ever-expanding higher education market. Organised around campus plans, specialist teaching and research buildings and constructions that act as a focus to academic life, the examples are drawn from around the world. In several cases different university buildings from the same architect are included to illustrate either the consistency or diversity of the approach the practice brings to specific design problems. To place the academic architecture in context, the introduction examines the growth and development of universities over time, with particular focus on the philosophical ideas that underpin our conception of contemporary higher education. Having analysed the radical changes that have taken place in this field towards the end of the 20th-century, the introduction ends by speculating on the form universities might take in the next millennium.

First let us address the issue of what a university is for.

FOR THE LOVE OF WISDOM

The very root of what a university is can be traced as far back as man's earliest search for knowledge, that most fundamental urge to comprehend, measure and in some way control his environment.

Indeed, from his most primitive beginnings man has sought to explain the world that is his experience. The first representations of the human experience date from Palaeolithic times, some 35,000 years ago. The images at Altamira and Laxcaux depict scenes painted on, or sculpted into, rock faces deep in inaccessible caves. They are extraordinarily lifelike, and portray not only animals, such as bison or stag, but also landscapes and scenes of people dancing or performing collective, perhaps ritualistic, acts.

Many theories have been put forward as to the purpose or meaning of these paintings. Do they depict fertility rights or are they perhaps intended to promote plentiful hunting? Or do they show mystical or magical offerings to unknown gods? However, fundamental to all these theories is the sense that our distant ancestors were in some way attempting to comprehend, even influence, the world in which they found themselves.

In our day, the quest to derive meaning from our existence was most elegantly described by the late Carl Sagan in his introduction to Stephen Hawking's *A Brief History of Time*:

> We go about our daily lives understanding almost nothing of the world. We give little thought to the machinery that generates the sunlight that makes life possible, to the gravity that glues us to an Earth that would otherwise send us spinning off into space, or to the atoms of which we are made and on whose stability we fundamentally depend. Except for children (who don't know enough not to ask the important questions), few of us spend much time wondering why nature is the way it is; where the cosmos came from, or whether it was always here; if time will one day flow backward and effects precede causes; or whether there are ultimate limits to what humans can know. There are even children, and I have met some of them, who want to know what a black hole looks like; what is the smallest piece of matter; why we remember the past and not the future; how it is, if there was chaos early, that there is, apparently, order today; and why there is a universe.

Using the most advanced technological instruments of man's creation, Sagan and Hawking search the depths of space for an explanation. Their quest is driven by the same, most primitive, human need that drove our distant ancestors to paint their world: the need to uncover what human beings can know. An essentially philosophical quest, it stems from that adjective's etymology: the Greek *philo* meaning love and *sophos* meaning wisdom.

THE SCHOOLS OF PLATO AND ARISTOTLE

The deliberate examination of knowledge begins with the great philosopher Plato some 2,400 years ago. It is his writings that provide us with the first systematic analysis and methodology whereby human questioning and understanding of the world could be structured. Plato started from a simple premise: 'Philosophy begins with wonder.' This idea, that wonder and investigation are fundamental to the nature of mankind, is at the heart of all universities today and the promotion of knowledge and the encouragement of human enquiry remain central.

Plato's search for knowledge was based on ascertaining the validity of explanations in a relentless search for absolute truth. His methodology was that of dialectic process, presenting theories and testing them against counterpropositions. Sir Karl Popper later restated the method as one of conjecture and refutation. The goal of achieving absolute certainty is common to all aspects of education and research worldwide.

Plato used a structure of conversations or dialogues between advocates of opposing ideas. Often these exchanges would take place in social circumstances, and it is from the Greek word for dinner party that we derive the word 'symposium'.

In ancient Greece the idea that man was able to attain insight into his world through the use of his own cognitive powers led to the single greatest expansion in human understanding that there has ever been. In 387 BC Plato founded the Academy, sometimes described as the first university. 'The academy' was simply the name of his house; there he would receive students for the purpose of discussion and argument. Among the olive groves of ancient Greece, Plato orchestrated not a syllabus of accepted knowledge and facts, but rather a method of enquiry. This method encouraged an attitude of thinking for oneself in a community bent on mutual exploration in the pursuit and development of knowledge. Again, a principle that is seminal to all university establishments today.

The most famous of Plato's students was Aristotle. He studied at the Academy for 20 years and went on to become tutor to Alexander the Great.

Aristotle's approach to understanding the world differed from Plato's. While his master had looked to an idealised world that was, as it were, behind the phenomena of experiences, Aristotle sought an explanation rooted in the experiences themselves. His method was based on a system of categorising the various aspects of human experience. By ordering the aspects of man's enquiry he established a structure of distinct disciplines within which investigation could be focused. It is to Aristotle that we owe much of our structure of knowledge; and from his books devoted to different subjects we gain the disciplines of logic, physics, economics, psychology, metaphysics, meteorology, rhetoric and ethics. An encyclopedist by nature, Aristotle went on to develop further categories and subsets of these disciplines

and, in so doing, provided the intellectual organising structure of the faculties, departments and areas of study familiar in our own universities.

Like Plato before him, Aristotle founded a school to promote teaching and enquiry. Called the Lyceum, it was situated outside Athens close to the temple of Apollo Lyceus. It took the form of a gymnasium and garden with covered walks. Aristotle used to stroll through the garden as he taught, a habit that gave his school the name Peripatetic from the Greek word *peripatetikos* meaning walking about. Peripatetics is now used to describe teachers who work in more than one place of learning. Of these first universities little remains today and we have to reconstruct much of their physical form from texts. In the dense suburbs of modern Athens the site of Plato's Academy is now a children's playground, while Aristotle's Lyceum has been recently uncovered and is now the subject of archaeological investigations. In both cases the schools were relatively short-lived and focused around the teachings of their respective masters. Hence it is clear that, other than in their important educational methods and structures, they bear little relationship to what we currently understand as a university, particularly in its physical sense.

Following the fall of Rome and the descent of classical civilisation into the Dark Ages, education took on a radically different form. With the rise of Christianity the emphasis the ancient Greeks had placed upon man's ability to understand and explain the world through his own powers of enquiry and reasoning was replaced by a new kind of teaching based on a divine explanation for human experience set out in a few key texts. This approach, known as scholasticism from the Greek word *skolastikos* meaning studious, would dominate Western thinking and education for more than nine centuries. The enquiry of medieval scholars was limited to the preservation and interpretation of God-given scriptures. In an uncertain world dominated by the threat of barbarian invasion, the task of preserving the divine texts, the scriptures, and their keepers, and handing them down to future generations drove the repositories to the extremities of the known world.

Not until the 13th-century, with the translation of Aristotle's texts, which had been preserved in Arabic, into Latin and their reinterpretation by such luminaries as Thomas Aquinas, did a new confidence begin to emerge that would place the wonder of human enquiry based on man's ability to reason back at the centre of academic endeavour.

THE MEDIEVAL UNIVERSITIES
The development of the university during the Middle Ages is closely linked to the establishment and growth of craft guilds. While the scholastic world had attended to the preservation of

scriptures, the secular world had developed a structure of practical education through the grouping together of trades and other commercial activities in the form of guilds. Craft guilds or *collegia* had existed since the time of imperial Rome, in the form of groups of people with common interests who wished to establish their status and preserve it from outside influences. Of the various guilds many are familiar today, such as masons and jewellers. Established to preserve and pass on their skills they developed ways of educating young men and admitting them to their group. Central to this was the system of apprenticeship. In parallel with the Church's protection and handing down of scriptures, the guilds handed down the skills of a pre-established body of knowledge. Young men were apprenticed to masters in order to learn by example the skills of their trade. Following this initial training they often travelled as journeymen to various places of work where they could further refine their skills and extend their knowledge through different experiences. On completion of these stages the apprentice/journeymen could attempt to prove his skills through the production of a 'masterpiece', satisfactory examination of which by his peers would lead to entry and membership of the guild. Membership enabled him to ply his trade and in turn qualified him to teach his craft, taking on apprentices in his own right.

At first guilds grew as voluntary groupings of people who shared common interests. These gradually evolved into regulatory bodies that ensured levels of competence among their members. By establishing standards and methods of training the guilds sought to protect their status in society and, in part, to monopolise their marketplace. In formalising these processes certain protections of title were established, initially by common recognition and later through legislation.

In order to identify its particular status each guild adopted rites of passage from apprenticeship through to master, with individuals 'admitted' to join the respective ranks. A series of rituals and customary regales were developed to mark the progression.

In the nonsecular world most education was concerned with the induction of novices to the priesthood, hence the development of cathedral schools and monasteries with predominantly theological educational agendas. One of the foremost of the cathedral schools was Chartres, outside Paris. Its origins date back to the 4th-century and the town had established itself as a centre of learning before construction of the great Gothic cathedral started at the end of the 11th-century. The subject of study was primarily the relationship between the scriptures and Greek philosophy, from a particular Neo-Platonic perspective. This involved, for example, the comparison and resolution of the creation story in

the book of Genesis and that described by Plato in the *Timaeus*.

Towards the end of the 13th-century the growth of towns and cities conflated the activities of the guilds with those of theological schooling. Which in turn led to the emergence of the first universities as we know them. Today we might identify a university as a place of learning and research, a community of students and teachers or a collection of buildings. The medieval Latin word *universitas* meant a corporation, society or community of any kind, made up of individuals sharing a common interest and having independent legal status. *Universitas* did not refer to the universality of learning and could denote any group such as a craft guild or municipal corporation.

The terms *stadium generale* is probably closer than *universitas* to our modern understanding of a university. *Stadium* denotes the idea of a school or place of learning, while *generale* refers not to the range of subjects studied but rather to the diversity of students and teachers that it attracts. The idea of such an institution was premised on the coming together of disparate individuals as a collective body.

But why should these people wish to associate with each other, and to what end? At the simplest level, one purpose was evidently the dissemination of knowledge through sharing experiences and ideas. And beyond this diffusion of existent knowledge there was the fundamental wish to advance understanding and the limits of knowledge itself. The search, or research, into human understanding does not simply mean discovering new things and the earliest universities sought to provide a context in which the spirit of enquiry and investigation could be promoted and cultivated.

To reiterate, from Plato came the theoretical structure for learning, and from that categorisation we derive the faculties, disciplines and curricula familiar in universities today. Plato's pupil Aristotle sought to develop the various branches of knowledge, a practice which became increasingly refined during the Middle Ages. Central to this development was the recognition of the seven liberal arts, divided into two realms: first, the subjects of grammar, logic and rhetoric, together known as the *trivium*; and second, the *quadrivium* comprising arithmetic, geometry, astronomy and music. Added to these at times were two further subjects; medicine and architecture. To medieval scholars the *trivium* and the *quadrivium* represented the two principal instruments of philosophy: the mind was enlightened and informed by the former and found expression in the latter.

The importance of the seven liberal arts is most clearly demonstrated in the right-hand bay of the royal portal at Chartres cathedral. Here scholars who best illustrate a particular art represent each discipline. Sculpted in the archivolt on the left-hand side, Euclid represents geometry, Cicero, rhetoric and Aristotle dialectic. On the right-hand side arithmetic is represented by boethius, astronomy by Ptolemy, music by Pythagoras and grammar by the figure of Donatus or Priscian. The context and purpose of the arts is also clearly illustrated in the placing of Mary and Child, representing wisdom incarnate, placed as the central figures in the tympanum. They are the focus and perfection of all human intellectual endeavour.

In the 12th-century Chartres was renowned for attempting to ascribe equal emphasis to each of the seven liberal arts as the ideal foundation for education. However, this theoretical goal of educational balance was rarely achieved and varying emphases were placed on parts of the *trivium* and *quadrivium*, to the extent that some subjects disappeared from the curriculum. However, it was generally accepted that the *trivium* was the elementary level of study, equivalent to reading for our Bachelor of Arts degree, and the *quadrivium* the higher division of the liberal arts equal to Master status. From this hierarchy we derive the word 'trivial'.

With the rediscovery of Aristotle's writings, the disciplines of dialectic and logic took on a new importance. There was change in thinking from scholastic acceptance of divinely given unquestionable knowledge to a new-found confidence in the ability of man to engage in creative enquiry that could reveal truths through systematic analysis.

UNIVERSITY ARCHITECTURE

Early medieval universities are the educational prototypes for our modern institutions. However, in their physical manifestations they were quite different. As described, their genesis was the coming together of people with a common aim and their meetings were initially serviced by an ad hoc arrangement of rented rooms or 'halls'. These first-generation universities were very much an integrated part of their host cities and towns. As the influence grew, the establishment of colleges associated with residential groupings of scholars and students emerged, so producing identifiable territories. The important issue is that the universities grew within the cities or towns. While today we can recognise particular territories in the form of colleges. In Oxford or Cambridge they developed progressively with the growing urban fabric.

In the United Kingdom only Oxford and Cambridge date from the 13th-century. From the 15th to the 19th-centuries students and scholars seeking a university education elsewhere had to travel either to Scotland (St Andrews founded 1410; Glasgow, 1451; Aberdeen, 1494 and Edinburgh, 1583), or Ireland and Trinity College, Dublin (founded 1591). Only in the mid-to-late 19th century was there any significant expansion in the foundation of new universities in England and Wales.

EARLY AMERICAN UNIVERSITIES

Preceding university expansion in Britain, the early American universities had begun to develop a new typology for the learning environment. Harvard is America's oldest academic institution, having been founded in 1637. Along with Princeton and Yale it developed within the Oxbridge typology, its environment centred on hall buildings and residential colleges. The concept of a unified campus plan began to emerge at William and Mary College, Williamsburg, Virginia, and also at Union College, Schenectady, New York. However, the major initiative in university planning and organisation was to come from Thomas Jefferson.

JOHN LOCKE

The progenitor of Jefferson's thinking and the man responsible for much of the growth in education that has occurred from the late 19th-century until today was the fountainhead of empirical philosophy: John Locke (1632–1704). Politician and social reformer, Locke's masterpiece, *Essay on the Nature of Human Understanding*, questioned the accepted wisdom about the way in which we learn. His, at the time revolutionary, view was that we are born with no a priori knowledge. By this he meant that we have no innate ideas or abilities, that our minds are a blank sheet of paper, or *tabula rasa*, upon which experience writes. Locke proposed that by generalising from our experience, a process termed 'induction', we are able to formulate theories about our world. These provide us with sufficient, yet never absolute, explanations that enable us to act in meaningful and productive ways.

Locke concluded that we are all equal at birth and that our future development is dependent upon the nature and variety of our experiences along with the attention we give to the relationships between, and explanations of, these phenomena – in effect, our education. This marked a liberal revolution in education which occurred in parallel with the revolution in experimental science inspired by Newton and others. For the first time since the ancient Greeks man had the confidence to believe that his own powers of observation and rational enquiry were the prime mechanisms for reaching an understanding of his world.

Locke's belief that we all have the potential for development and self-betterment is now one of the cornerstones of university teaching. His idea that our potential is not limited by innate characteristics deriving from our social or cultural backgrounds stands as one of the governing principles of democratic societies the world over. It is therefore not surprising that his most immediate influence would be on one of the youngest countries faced with establishing a structure based on such liberal ideals. So it is that when the founding fathers of the United States of America penned the first constitution it was John Locke's innovative thinking that they enshrined.

THOMAS JEFFERSON AND THE UNIVERSITY OF VIRGINIA

Following on from Locke's liberal ideas, Thomas Jefferson instituted a major departure in educational philosophy with new legislation which provided a state university system, which in turn led to the founding of the University of Virginia.

Jefferson was not only a revolutionary educational thinker but also a statesman, lawyer and ambassador – and third president of the United States. In addition, he was a talented amateur architect and his design for the campus of the University of Virginia represented a new paradigm for the structuring of a university, its planning and operation.

His vision is notable in his use of the classical canon and its interpretation via Andrea Palladio's *Quattro Libri*. For Jefferson the adoption of the classical order was more than a matter of stylistic preference; his deployment of the architectural grammar of the ancients indicated a clear aspiration to associate his new democratic educational politics with those of the classical world, albeit he explicitly denied the relevance of the great classical thinkers. But Jefferson's great achievement was to combine these ideas with the concept of a liberal democracy, through an egalitarian planning system and the creation of a campus architecture. Inspired by the Renaissance ideas of Palladio, the pavilion in the landscape evoked the clarity and potential of man's rational understanding in contrast to the chaos of the natural world.

To achieve this ideal academic environment Jefferson devised a series of pavilions arranged around a great public space called 'the lawn'. This formed the focus of what he termed an 'academic village' leading to the promotion of an 'academic community'. The population of the community would live as families with each villa the residence of a tutor (professor), with lodgings above and a hall below for classes. Each villa differed slightly from the next in appearance, thus reflecting the individual nature of the group to which it belonged. Importantly, each lodging was connected to the next by means of a covered walkway, extending the idea of an individual collegiate model but within an overarching unitary university.

Central to this composition was the rotunda. Modelled on the Pantheon and in part borrowing references from Bouelé's cenotaph to Sir Isaac Newton, the building occupies the focal position on the campus. Accommodating lecture rooms, library and other communal areas it represents the intellectual heart of Jefferson's campus design and symbolises his educational ideals.

Jefferson's model of a clearly defined academic community premised on a heterogeneous campus was repeated across much of North America in the state university system and grew to be the predominant typology for new universities worldwide. Most notably this occurred in the development and planning strategies adopted for the rapid expansion of universities at the beginning of the 20th-century and during the expansion in higher education after the Second World War.

In England the establishment of new universities was a relatively modest affair during the 19th-century with Durham in 1832, London in 1836, Manchester in 1860 and Cardiff in 1893. Of these, University College London is significant for the educational insight and change brought about by one man: Jeremy Bentham. Although only one of a group who founded the university, Bentham is today remembered as a radical educational and social reformer. Discouraged by the educational and religious dogma of Oxford and Cambridge, he sought an educational environment that would encourage greater freedom of thought. Founded on a belief that the interests of the individual are at one with those of society, the philosophy Bentham developed premised a utility in the application of knowledge. The unbiased pragmatism and equality of his ideas is today enshrined in University College London's mission statement:

> To continue its founders' vision by providing educational opportunities of the highest quality to all, regardless of background.

An enigmatic character in his lifetime Bentham's presence in the university continues most literally today, with his embalmed body dressed in his normal clothes seated in a glass case in the entrance hall.

THE EXPANSION OF UNITED KINGDOM HIGHER EDUCATION THROUGH THE 20TH CENTURY

In the United Kingdom academic institutions were established in Sheffield in 1905, Leeds in 1904, Liverpool in 1903, Belfast in 1908 and Bristol in 1909, but thereafter the social and economic influences of two world wars largely brought the development of such educational buildings to a halt.

It is the universities mentioned above, along with their predecessors and new universities, that are often referred to as 'redbrick', grouping together institutions other than those of Oxford and Cambridge, London and Scotland. These redbrick foundations, so called not only because of the predominant architectural style of the times but also as a representation of a less ostentatious manner of education, mark the second generation of university institutions and a conscious move away from the grandeur and social privilege of Oxford and Cambridge's ancient and venerable spires. Their construction also represented a change in the automatic progression of the country's elite from public school to Oxbridge education that had persisted for the past 500 years. The purpose of these new universities was to provide a far more equal access to higher education. So it was that most of the first generation of municipal-school graduates was born from their intake.

London universities remained somewhat unusual in having a broad national and international intake. This was, of course, synonymous with their location in the capital. Others at the time tended to draw their intake by dint of their geographical and regional status.

At their inception the redbrick universities were seen as technical establishments concerned with the more pragmatic issues of everyday life, and with preparing a few students for entrance to the London external degrees. Yet from a slow and painful start these institutions began to show themselves as different from, yet equal to, their Oxbridge counterparts, establishing specialisms and expertise in their own right. And through this they won their own university status, enabling them to award their own degrees.

The greatest expansion in university education in the United Kingdom came in the decade from 1960 to 1970. The Robbins Report of 1963 recommended a yet greater extension of higher education than was already under way. Over that decade the number of British universities more than doubled, from 22 to 46 institutions, while the publication in 1966 of the government white paper *A Plan for Polytechnics and Other Colleges* meant that around 30 polytechnics were formed from existing colleges and higher education institutions. It was intended that the polytechnics would differ from traditional universities in that they would offer greater access to part-time students and their courses would be arranged equally around degree and vocational studies. Initially, they were not afforded university college status and hence were not able to award their own degrees. Later an overarching Council for the National Academic Awards was established to provide the regulatory framework for, and award degree-giving powers to, the polytechnics. As a result of the ensuring explosion in student numbers, the CNAA was eventually awarding more degrees than all the collegiate universities put together. In 1991 the government white paper *Higher Education, a New Framework* announced that polytechnics were to be given degree-awarding powers and university titles, within a new united funding system of education.

To accommodate the expansion of new universities that occurred between 1960 and 1970 many new, greenfield campuses were constructed, including the foundations of East Anglia, Sussex, Essex and Warwick. Like Jefferson's at Virginia 150 years earlier these new institutions, presented with a *tabula rasa* in respect of their design, posed a unique challenge for architects. They marked the third generation of university expansion and their growth was meteoric, with student numbers exceeding 3,000 at each institution within a decade of establishment.

Piecemeal generic growth had been largely representative of expansion in higher education in the United Kingdom until then and the architects of the new universities were faced with a problem of masterplanning and social engineering – central to which was how rapid growth could be managed through staged implementation of a strategic plan. Writing in the *Architectural Review* in October 1963, Lionel Brett opined that the approach varied quite radically between the architects, who were working on what were effectively similar projects in terms of programme and scale, but on isolated greenfield sites. He concluded that there were three identifiable design strategies, which derived from the architect's view of the way in which growth would be managed.

Sir Basil Spence's scheme for the University of Sussex represented the *campus* model. A strongly identified core building would provide the starting point from which the campus structure plan would extend outwards. Spence established this strong identity using a system of precast concrete vaults and brick construction evocative of Le Corbusier's Maison Jaoul. Of the two buildings in the initial phase, the physics building and Falmer House, the latter accommodates students' rooms, the refectory and the debating chamber. It takes the form of a quadrangle with a central courtyard and represents the social and intellectual core of the campus. However, the inevitable problem with such a strategy is that the central focus is caught between being too large at the beginning of the concentric expansion and too small at the conclusion of the expansion. In addition, as has been the case at Sussex, an initial planning strategy intended to maintain a certain visual consistency in archi-tectural grammar has been changed with the progression of time, according to the changing nature and requirements of higher education and the appointment of other architects. Accordingly, the initial clarity of intent represented by the pioneer buildings has been somewhat swamped by a less visually consistent range of additions. This may be considered either as being detrimental to the overall cohesion of the plan or, as is the case with Eric Parry's building featured in the following case studies, as providing the opportunity for exceptional new architecture.

Assessing the design of architects Robert Mathew, Johnson-Marshall and Partners for the University of York, Brett detected what he termed the *molecular* campus. Derived from the Oxbridge collegiate model, its structure plan established several social nuclei centred around a tripartite grouping of functions comprised of the following: two colleges; a dedicated building function, for example, a science teaching or research building; and one of the buildings of general function, for example, hall, library, theatre, etc. The strategy sought to overlay different activities of the expanding university in parallel around these mixed-use foci. The site for York was developed very much in the English Picturesque tradition: an undulating topography, irregularity of planting and an artificial winding lake presented a Repton landscape. The Picturesque approach lent itself to the erection of individual pavilions juxtaposed in the landscape. However, this individualised building expression was contrasted with the use of a standardised component building system across the various colleges.

The third planning type to accommodate growth came from Denys Lasdun's design for the University of East Anglia and was termed the *concentrated* model. The most important aspect of the development strategy was the proposed academic structure. The university was to be unitary, and organised around schools of study that would provide the academic and social structure. Creating identifiable colleges or faculty buildings was discouraged in favour of implementing a building system that obscured autonomous disciplines in favour of blurred academic boundaries. Lasdun's response was to devise a building 'organism' comprising a linear arrange-ment, or wall, of neutral teaching accommodation facing which was a chain of student residences connected by a narrow access route. The residential units were organised along the lines of Oxbridge college halls with 12 students sharing common facilities. The groups of rooms are arranged in a cascading ziggurat-like structure that overlooks a river and open fields beyond.

The models identified above, while unique to campus planning, were in no way innovative in terms of urban planning strategies and the questions they pose for architects are central to much urban planning theory. What is unique, however, is that faced with the same problem at the same point in time architects from broadly similar backgrounds should independently generate three contrasting models. At the root of each response is the question of how much control any one architect can hope to achieve in the design of such a complex structure as a university. Campus planning presents an age-old architectural enigma as to how much control can,

or indeed should, be exercised. Basil Spence was at one time quite at ease with loose architectural structure, saying of the Sussex campus that he:

> … welcomed the idea of incompleteness as a virtue, incomplete-ness was life itself. It was in that mind that the first designs were done.

Yet he could not really give up the idea of his own vision, going on to say:

> I saw the University now and in the future in pink brick with some arched forms peeping in the trees.

Of course, other architects have been less candid in their search for overall control and uniformity in campus planning and design. Depending on political imperatives, campus architecture can be a means of achieving ideological change. Such was the case at the Illinois Institute of Technology where Mies van de Rohe was commissioned to design a campus of authoritarian Modernist dogma in order to 'correct' an educational establishment that was thought to have lost its way. As the *Architectural Record* reported at the time, Mies was hired to, 'lead without fail to a clear and unequivocal spiritual orientation'. This he clearly did in the creation of an uncompromising campus and educational structure. It has been observed that dogma even extended to the orthogonal precision of the alignment of drawing boards in the School of Architecture. The 'Mies School' was in effect the antithesis of Plato's ancient educational objective of encouraging students to think for themselves.

The elevation of polytechnics and other colleges to the status of universities has promoted a fourth generation of universities. Generally located within an urban context, these new establishments have grown as individual colleges with allegiance not to each other but rather to the civic institutions to which they relate. Much like their medieval guild predecessors, they have made the link between everyday life and the world of academic investigation and research a vital part of civic life. In a context of global information exchange these locally based schools benefit from the possibilities of an international guild form of networking. Hence, the third generation of isolated campuses is being challenged by a network of higher education institutions, based locally yet able to think globally. We stand at the dawn of a new age in higher education.

THE FOUR AGES OF UNIVERSITIES

In mapping the history of universities since the Middle Ages one can identify four distinct architectural generations. Examples of the first generation are the universities of Paris, Bologna, Oxford and Cambridge, all integral to their host cities. Christopher Alexander, a veteran of several departments and educational institutions, has commented that in Cambridge this growth is so ingrained with that of the city that,

> At certain points Trinity Street is physically almost indistinguishable from Trinity College. The buildings on the street, though they contain stores and coffee shops and banks at ground level, contain undergraduates' rooms above in their upper storeys. In many cases the actual fabric of the street buildings melts into the fabric of the old college so that one cannot be altered without the other.

While Alexander describes this overlapping of academic and commercial activities as being of merit, it is also true that, like Cambridge, some cities have come to be dominated by the university and its interests. Here the balance between civic and academic life has been altered to such an extent that the city lives through its university.

The advent of the second, redbrick, generation of universities marked an opening up of education through regionally based institutions. At first these prepared candidates for the traditional examinations, but over the course of time they developed their own expertise and award-granting status.

In contrast to the model of university and city growing together within the urban matrix, the third generation of universities sought a physical containment from their host cities through the establishment of out-of-town campuses. This development was the result of a postwar explosion in access to higher education and a commensurate need rapidly to establish new institutions, and embodied Jefferson's idea of the academic village, autonomous in its location and operation. In cases such as Sussex, East Anglia and York the city has developed according to its own commercial agenda and acts only as a kind of service vehicle for the academic satellite. Paraphrasing Donald Schon's metaphor of architectural practice, this model presents a particular physical and intellectual topography – that of a high, hard ground overlooking a swamp. On the high ground stands the idealised world of study and research where identifiable problems lend themselves to solutions through research-based theory and methods. In contrast, in the swampy lowlands lies the complex day-to-day world of other human activities where problems are messy and confusing and incapable of technical solution.

Schon describes the irony of divorcing everyday life from the world of academia. The problems on much of the high ground seem rarefied and relatively unimportant to individuals and society at large, however great their technical interest, while in the swamp lie the problems of greatest human concern. Hence, while intellectually the application of research to the world of everyday affairs is an issue for all

universities, no matter what their history or physical location, the autonomous campus has served only to reinforce this perceived separation.

The fourth generation of universities, today in its infancy, marks recognition of the fact that many institutions undertake higher-educational roles to the same standards as the established universities. In addition, changes in funding structures and the population's expectations regarding access to higher education, and the advent of global education, have done much to encourage established institutions to reappraise their traditional role.

Universities now see themselves moving from being providers of only full-time education, towards becoming establishments that offer specific academic awards. Greater access to higher education has encouraged methods of part-time or distance-based learning techniques. Associated with these developments has been the emphasis on credit accumulation and transfer, which enables students to negotiate their education from a variety of providers. In this consumer-driven society of pick and mix from various educational establishments, courses and components, a profound paradigmatic shift has occurred in the role that educational providers see themselves playing. The concept of lifelong learning has arisen in tandem with these changes, and to cater for this universities have developed portfolios of short courses often deriving from the full-time course syllabus.

The pedagogical structure of education has also undergone a revolution. The change from a teaching-based culture to a student-centred learning environment has brought new demands on the kinds of resources offered by universities. Libraries and seminar rooms have been replaced by learning resource centres; staff rooms and common rooms by e-mail addresses; and examination rooms by computer-aided assessment. What students expect from staff, and staff from students, has also changed. From being passive note-takers and receivers of given wisdom students have been encouraged towards (and perhaps have themselves encouraged) the adoption of a far more proactive role in their education. With increasing requirements of self-funding as a result of the pressures greater access has brought to bear on government resources, student expectations regarding the quality of education have changed. Today educational 'consumers' demand value and provision.

In just over a century, from 1889 to 1996, the annual government funding of United Kingdom universities increased from £15,000 to £7,000 million. The pattern of growth has been exponential with the rapidity dramatically increasing postwar and continuing to climb ever more steeply into the next millennium. Hence it is clear that we are increasingly moving towards a learning society. At the start of the 21st-century, knowledge and learning are a fundamental element of postmodern consumption.

No matter that at graduation ceremonies students and staff may array themselves in the cloak and mortarboard of 13th-century apparel, the reality of modern higher education represents a cataclysmic change that has had profound repercussions for university architects. Prestigious commissions for cash-rich Oxbridge colleges still persist, but on an intentional scale these are relatively insignificant. To meet the demands of increasing student numbers and changes in the nature of education, new universities need to commission a variety of new buildings and new building types. Educational structures have to embody the aspirations and status that the institutions wish to achieve and represent. New universities have quickly recognised the value and prestige that architecture can provide as an outward symbol of an educational body. Education is an invisible substance; architecture allows it to become material.

Like the Medici in Renaissance Florence, new universities can be seen as great architectural patrols at the start of the 21st-century. There is now widespread recognition that the requirement to provide aesthetically inspiring and highly functional environments has afforded extraordinary opportunities for architects to investigate and develop new types of buildings for education. Indeed, Joseph Rykwert identified the university as the archetypical building type for our era:

> Historical epochs might also be classified by the kind of building which is the archetype or paradigm – depending which way you are looking – to all that gets built in the age. That is what the temple was in ancient Greece; the city in general to republican, the baths alone to imperial Rome; the cathedral to the Middle Ages; the palace to the XVIIth century – and so on, until you came to the block of flats in the period 1920–40. And for us now it is the university.

Architecture has a powerful role in the messages a university wishes to send to its staff, students and the outside world. Lord St John of Fawsley identified the important symbolic role architecture had to play when he talked about Short and Ford's Queen's Building at De Montfort University:

> Architecture, particularly on a campus, can have symbolic power and provide a focal point for a university, particularly one that has been moulded from disparate buildings.

De Montfort University Queen's Building, the subject of a case study in this book, is particularly remarkable in this semiotic context. Building from his experiences with Rowe and Koetter at Harvard, Alan Chort has collaged a piece of 19th-century, late Gothic establishment architecture into a campus of system-built 1960s grid-planning. The effect is that of William

Butterfield meeting Mies van der Rohe's Illinois Institute of Technology. The contrast is dramatic.

Universities, and certainly university campuses, represent a kind of microcosm of the city. They comprise a variety of building types: instructional facilities, libraries and museums, research laboratories, institutional services, housing and sports and recreational facilities alongside buildings for extracurricular activities: churches, refectories, bars, shops and banks, even medical centres. A single volume cannot hope to cover all these building types across a range of educational establishments. Indeed, to cover one university such as Harvard would require a similar-sized publication.

The focus of the following case studies has accordingly been organised into a narrow band. We do not include university museums or libraries, already covered in other books in this series. Nor do we include residential buildings which, although a core aspect of the development and growth of universities, would need an entire publication for fair coverage and comparison.

The case studies are arranged in three areas of architectural interest that are key to the development of contemporary universities. First there are campus and structure plans – the manner in which an often diverse range of building typologies and functional requirements interrelates. We consider campuses not only as the autonomous second-generation universities, brilliantly reinvented by the Stirling Wilford partnership at Temasek University, Singapore. We also look at campus strategies as integral parts of their host city structure. Among these, Dixon and Jones's proposal for a new university in Croydon presents an ambitious model of the way in which town and gown can be overlaid to create the kind of architectural collage Christopher Alexander noted in Trinity Street, Cambridge.

Second, we look at individual specialist buildings that have arisen out of specific educational or research needs. The focus of this examination has been on the way in which similar buildings have sought to symbolise their individual functions as distinct elements in the university structure. Rather than a comprehensive catalogue of these building types – for example, those of medical research buildings another book in its own right – we have sought to present a range of these idiosyncratic structures.

Third, and allied to the original collegiate nature of universities, we analyse the collective spaces in which students and teachers come together across their respective disciplines. As university pedagogy moves from a teaching-towards a learning-based environment we look at the facilities that constitute a new typology of 'learning resource centres' around which many new and old universities are now focusing their building programmes. Examples of this are buildings such as that by the Richard Rogers Partnership at Slough, and the imaginative commission by Sir Colin Stansfield Smith with Hampshire County Architects for the University of Portsmouth. These structures mark a profound change of vision in that they provide nondedicated spaces, intended to accommodate technological advance and oriented around a diverse range of student learning needs.

UNIVERSITIES: THE FUTURE

The change in the pattern of teaching and learning that have engendered many of these new university buildings have occurred in symbiosis with equally dramatic changes in the technology used in higher education, particularly exponential advances in communication media. The use of such media has been an important aspect of the changes in education since early in the 20th-century. The use of radio to educate and inform a mass audience in the early 1920s and 1930s had as profound an effect as the development of printed material some 400 years previously. For example, two-way radio communication has allowed teachers to conduct classes with a 'classroom' of students scattered around the Australian outback on remote cattle stations. In the United Kingdom the Open University quickly developed the use of televisual communications.

The possibilities for distance-based learning which the Open University pioneered have been greatly enhanced by the advent of readily accessible network communication via the Internet. Electronic information exchange has begun a revolution in higher education that is today only in its infancy. The traditional role of the geographically determined university and campus will be transformed by the emergence of a global educational provision.

In his 1995 book *City of Bits; Space Place and the Infobahn* Professor Bill Mitchell, the long-standing architectural cyber guru from the Massachusetts Institute of Technology, speculated on the impact network communications would have on education:

> Network connections quickly create new ways of sharing knowledge and enacting practices and so force changes in the character of teaching spaces. At the very least, a lecture theatre now needs a computer workstation integrated with a podium and a computer connected video projector to supplement the old blackboards and slide projectors; the podium is no longer a place for reading from a book or lecturing from written notes, but a spot for directing and interpreting a stream of bits.
>
> Desktop-to-desktop, switched video networks open the more radical possibilities of teaching in virtual rather than physical settings. Students might have office conferences with faculty members without leaving their dormitory rooms. Seminars might be conducted without seminar rooms. Symposia might virtually assemble speakers from widely scattered locations. Lecturers might perform from distant places, and without the need to concentrate students in auditoriums.

He ends by commenting:

> As the twentieth century draws to a close, the idea of a virtual campus – paralleling or perhaps replacing the physical one – seems increasingly plausible. If a latter-day Jefferson were to lay out an ideal educational community for the third millennium, she might site it in cyberspace.

In the five years since Mitchell's book was published the plausibility of the virtual campus is no longer in doubt. The question is not whether such an institution will be realised, but rather when it will be. In all probability the inception of the virtual campus will not be through any single educational establishment but instead through one of the giant computer-software houses.

In the progression of British university development, from the medieval inception of Oxford and Cambridge to the second age of the expansion of redbrick universities then to the third age of the out-of-town campus plans of the 1960s and the fourth of the polytechnic universities as integrated parts of the city's fabric, we are now moving towards the virtual campus which will offer the fifth incarnation of the university. Let me conclude with a quotation from the pseudonymous author of *Red Brick Universities*, Bruce Truscot. He says of university students:

> When they go from university they should feel fuller, and yet emptier, than when they entered it; they should have an increased power, yet at the same time a keener sense of their own weaknesses; above all they should be afire with a passion to discover and explore.

In compiling the following case studies we have endeavoured to show the power that architecture at its best has to provide an environment that will contribute towards the nurturing of such a passion.

Mosaic depicting the School of Plato (courtesy of the Soprintendenza Archeologica delle Province di Napoli e Caserta, Italy)

TRINITY COLLEGE DUBLIN DENTAL HOSPITAL

Dublin, Ireland

Dublin Dental Hospital, which was founded in 1895, contains the School of Dental Science, one of the constituents of the Faculty of Health and Sciences at Trinity College, Dublin.

The façade of the original Victorian building on Lincoln Place has for along time been identified with the dental hospital and also, because it is in a conservation area, needed to be retained. For reasons of tradition, therefore, as well as economy, it was decided to retain the existing buildings on Lincoln Place, to refurbish them so that they form part of the new hospital complex and to enter the new hospital from Lincoln Place through the old building so maintaining the historic presence of the hospital. The new building occupies the site at the rear of the hospital within the Trinity College campus. (It was, however, necessary to persuade the planning authority to allow demolition of an existing addition on the site.)

We were therefore faced with the need to preserve the old buildings and to keep them operational as a hospital – this involved a highly complex interface – while erecting a new building on the site behind them:

'behind' seen from Lincoln Place, 'in front' seen from the college. The refurbished old building now mainly accommodates teaching areas for the dental school.

Most of the clinical functions of the hospital are located within the new building and are designed with appropriate spaces clear of structure, appropriate ceiling heights and suitable service distribution systems. The clinics are designed to be light and friendly in character and to reflect a balance of openness and privacy, order and informality.

The central atrium is a full-height space enclosed between the old and new buildings with a fully glazed roof; it contains the main stairs and lift as well as reception and waiting areas and bridge links between the two buildings at all levels. It is the circulation hub and unifies the building, both visually and functionally.

New floors are of reinforced concrete construction with steel frames used for roofs and within the old building. Externally, brick is used to tie in with the original hospital building. Granite cladding is used within the college in sympathy with the other buildings.

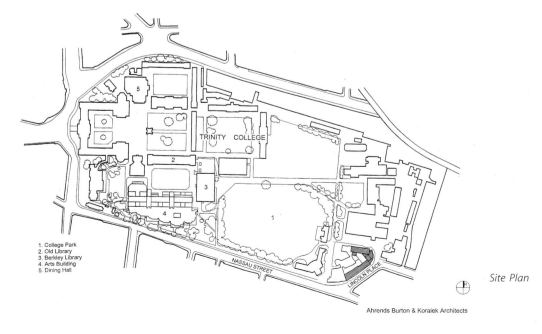

1. College Park
2. Old Library
3. Berkley Library
4. Arts Building
5. Dining Hall

Site Plan

Ahrends Burton & Koralek Architects

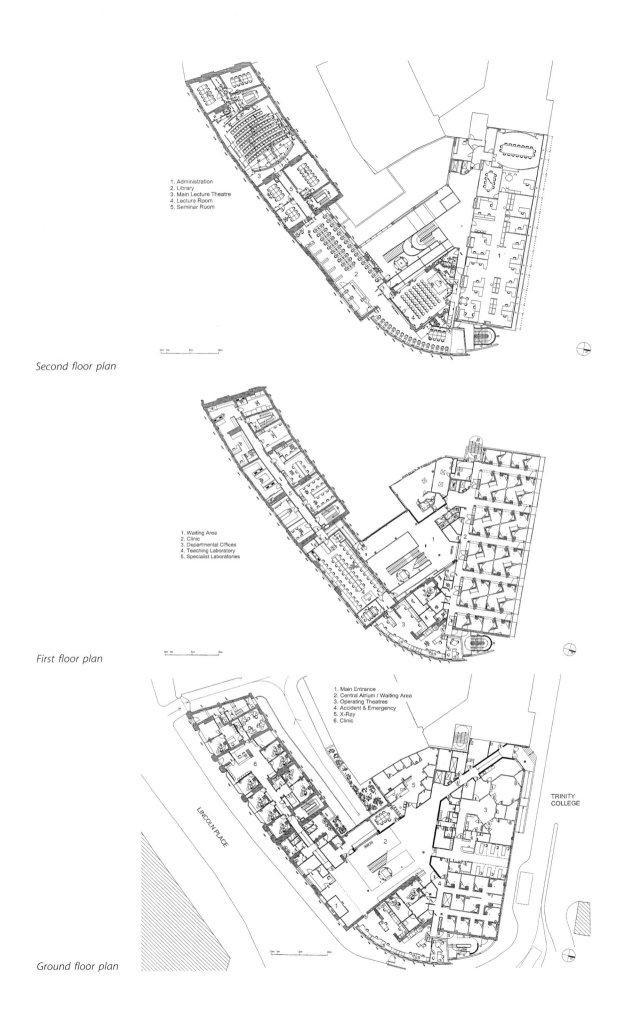

1. Administration
2. Library
3. Main Lecture Theatre
4. Lecture Room
5. Seminar Room

Second floor plan

1. Waiting Area
2. Clinic
3. Departmental Offices
4. Teaching Laboratory
5. Specialist Laboratories

First floor plan

1. Main Entrance
2. Central Atrium / Waiting Area
3. Operating Theatres
4. Accident & Emergency
5. X-Ray
6. Clinic

LINCOLN PLACE

TRINITY COLLEGE

Ground floor plan

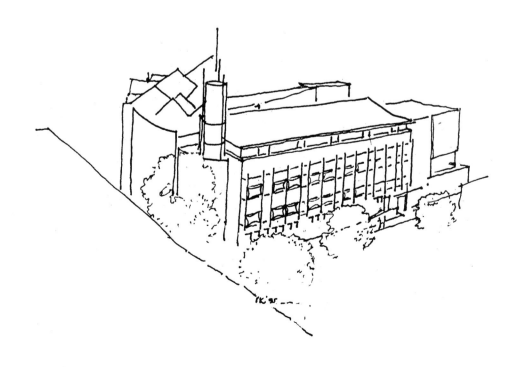

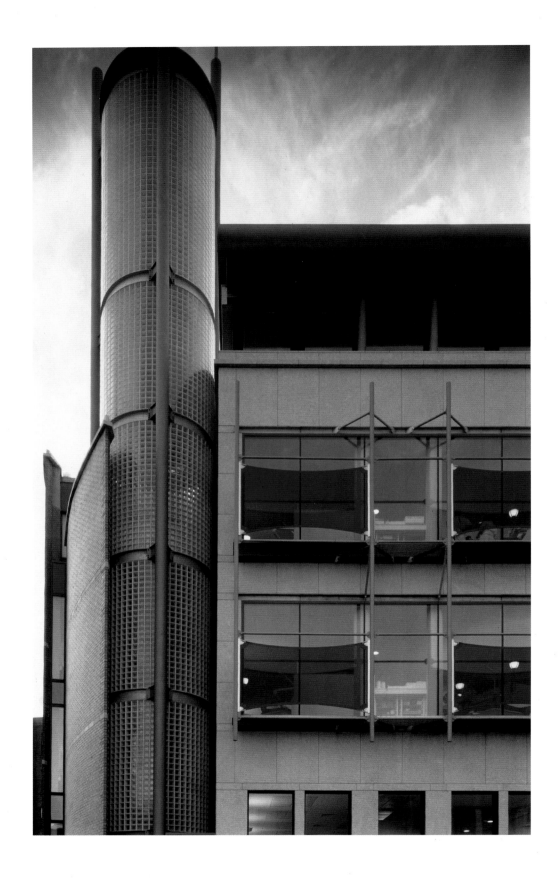

ALLIES AND MORRISON
UNIVERSITY OF SOUTHAMPTON STUDENT UNION
Southampton, United Kingdom

This new two-storey building houses Southampton University's student union shop and, on the upper floor, a wide top-lit gallery that serves three smaller retail units.

The siting of the building reinforces the existing network of pedestrian routes established by Sir Basil Spence's 1950s masterplan for the campus. Located adjacent to the existing student union, the new building helps to define a square to the front that marks the southern edge of the central university green which is faced by the building's brickwork north facade. The double-height portico to the new shop extends out into the square giving the union entrance an appropriate prominence and providing a sheltered meeting place, while three large timber-shuttered openings reveal the roof-lit public space at first-floor level.

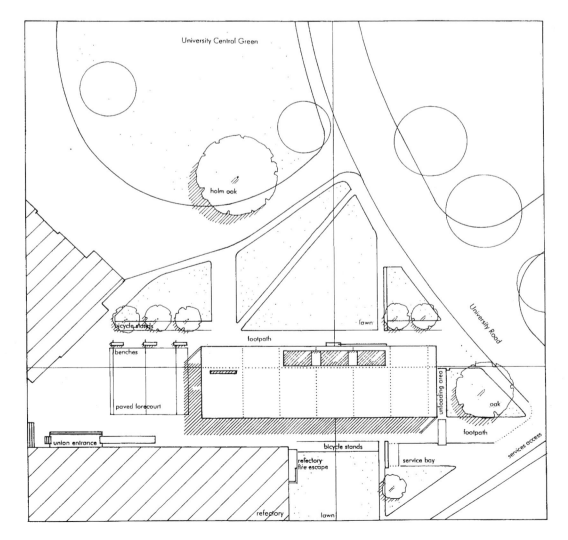

Site plan

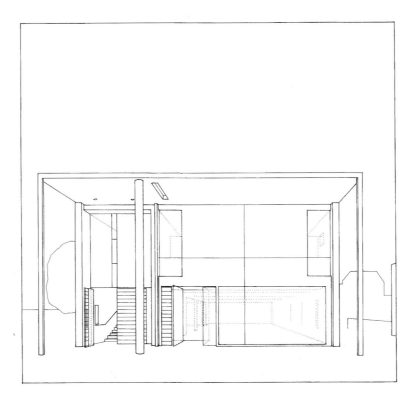

West elevation

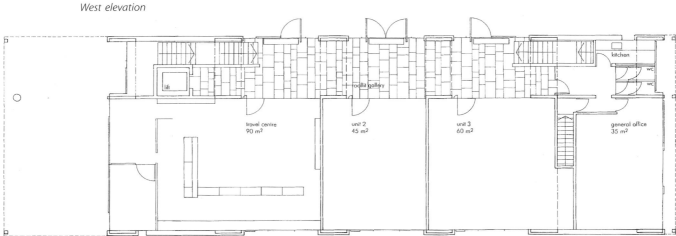

First floor plan

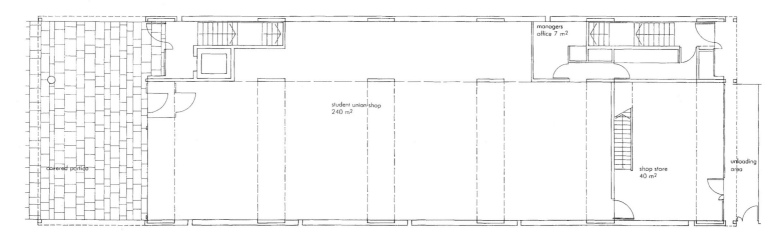

Ground floor plan

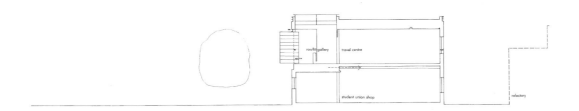

Section

PATRICK BERGER & JACQUES ANZIUTTI

MONTMUZARD UNIVERSITY
MAISON DE L'UNIVERSITÉ DE BOURGOGNE

Dijon, France

The Maison de l'Université, situated in the Montmuzard University campus, Dijon, is composed of two distinct parts, positioned one above the other and corresponding to the building's two main functions: first, a ground floor public in character, accommodating the *salle des actes* and a reception area; second, two upper levels, administrative and private in character, containing offices. The structure of the building and the arrangement of the volumes represent the two different orders: the institutional order of the ground floor and the administrative order of the floors above.

The ground floor is freed from structural supports. The spanning of this volume called for the creation of a technically individual structure, hence a reinforced concrete beam extends across the entire area and takes on the load of the two upper levels. In the great space on the ground floor freed up by the beam, and

crossing the building, is the *salle des actes*, which provides 150 seats. This structure is entirely of beech wood: floor, ceiling and walls. It is the representative face of the Maison de l'Université, and is conceived as an autonomous piece of architecture, presented on a stone floor.

The Maison de l'Université is enclosed by a facade of three materials: stone, wood and metal. Each material is used for a particular function: the stone is for the gables and the entrances and is similar to that used for the first buildings of the campus; the wood is employed for the opening parts: shutters/panels for the ventilation of the offices and for doors at the entrances to the building; and the metal is for the waterproofing of the facade, of the horizontal bands and the glazed frames.

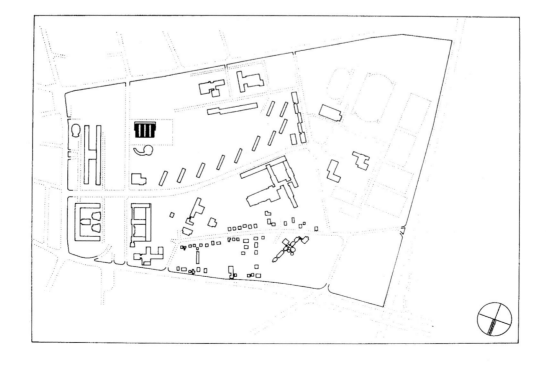

Site plan

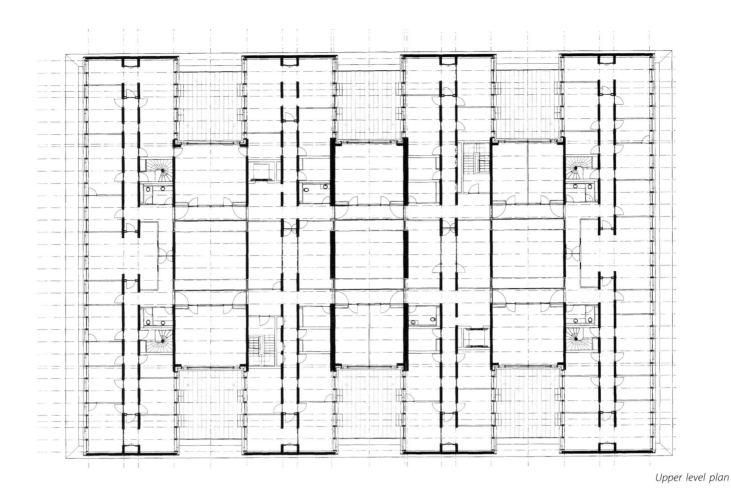

Upper level plan

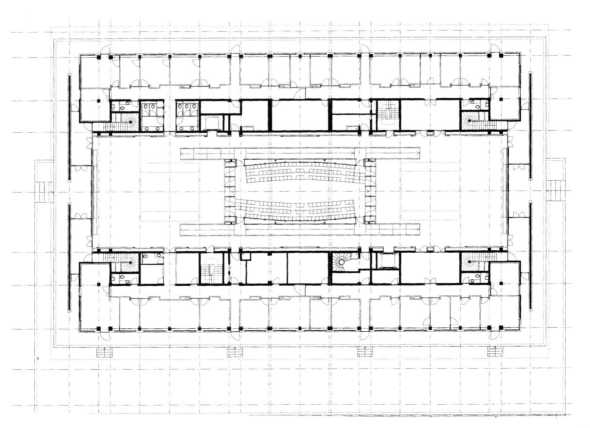

Ground floor plan

Section (north to south)

Section (east to west)

TRINITY COLLEGE ATRIUM AND DINING HALL

Dublin, Ireland

The 18th-century dining hall of Trinity College, Dublin, was almost destroyed by fire in 1984. This building complex where many social activities take place, houses the college's dining hall, kitchens, buttery, bars and senior common room. The aftermath of the fire presented the college with both a major task of restoration, and the opportunity to improve the hitherto piecemeal character of the complex.

Once the cloakrooms had been removed, the calm simplicity of the stone-flagged entrance hall was revealed. When the original dining-hall windows, which had been blocked by a modern extension, were replaced, the hall's central volume was flooded with natural light. A white Portland stone floor replaced the dark mahogany of the original, and oak tables and chairs were designed to furnish the space. The formally composed elevations of the new hall established an architectural promenade for diners.

The senior common room, situated above the entrance hall, was restored and refurbished with furniture inspired by 18th-century originals. The new four-storey oak-clad atrium links all levels of the building, and shutters enable its galleries to be enclosed as separate rooms or open out on to the space beneath. A small bar, for the Fellows' private use, re-creates the Adolf Loos Karntner Bar amid the ascetic Classicism of Irish Palladianism.

Other inventions improved the circulation. New stone staircases to the left and right of the entrance hall lead down to the buttery and cellars, and smaller meeting rooms, society rooms and service spaces are accommodated into the plan.

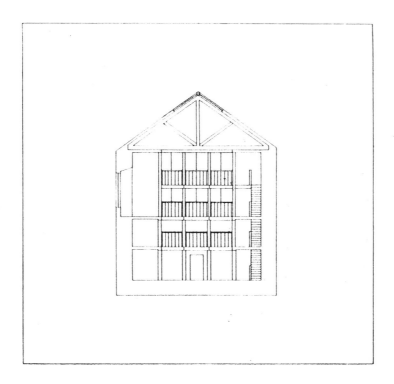

Section

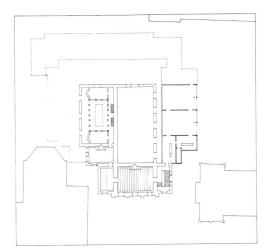

Second floor plan

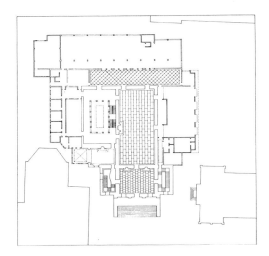

First floor plan

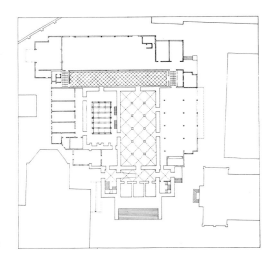

Ground floor plan

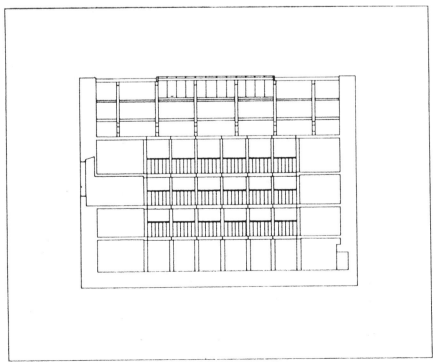

Section

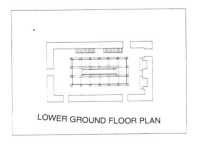

LOWER GROUND FLOOR PLAN

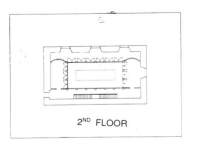

2ND FLOOR

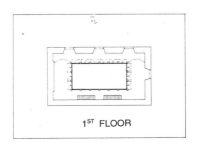

1ST FLOOR

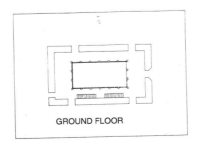

GROUND FLOOR

CORK INSTITUTE OF TECHNOLOGY LIBRARY

Cork, Ireland

Forming the first phase of a three-part programme of construction, the library covers an area of 2,250m², with a further 450m² of gallery space, and can accommodate 70,000 volumes and up to 500 students. To a large extent materials traditional to the area were used, in particular clay bricks and white limestone. These are contrasted with oak-and-glass screens and flush-jointed concrete blockwork. The reading room is lit by a north-facing rooflight over the main circulation route, the gallery spaces by floor-to-ceiling windows.

Internally, extensive use is made of segmental arches which, like the columns, are brick faced, the bricks serving as permanent shuttering for the reinforced concrete core. The recesses between columns were used to accommodate various furnishing elements such as book shelves along the curving south wall. Further reading facilities were installed and are lit by groups of three small windows which form the only openings in this face.

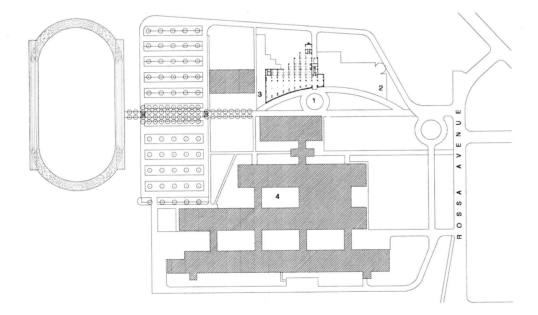

Campus plan:
1. New library
2. Proposed second phase
3. Proposed third phase
4. Existing college

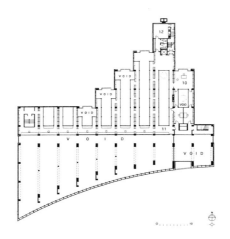

Second floor plan:
10. Librarian's Office
11. Reserved Books
12. Staff Room

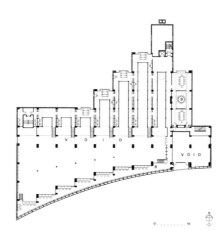

First floor plan:
8. Periodicals Library
9. Classrooms

Ground floor plan:
1. Entrance
2. Desk
3. Librarians' Hall
4. Passage
5. Reading Room
6. Book Stacks
7. Accessioning

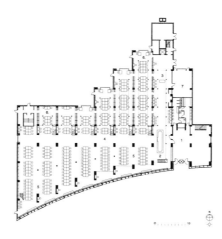

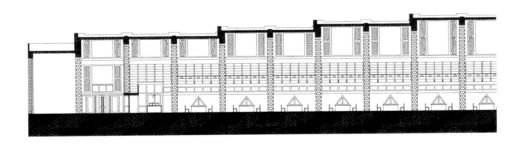

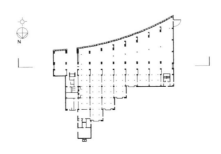

*Section through long
passage of Library*

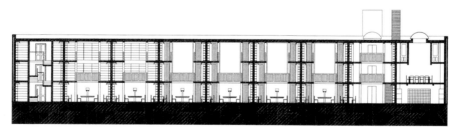

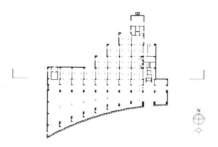

Section through Book Stacks

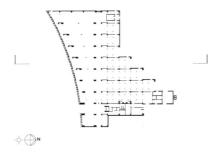

Section through Forecourt, Reading Room and Book Stacks

DE BLACAM & MEAGHER
CLUAIN MHUIRE SCHOOL OF ART
Galway, Ireland

The School of Art is located in a former seminary built for the Redemptorist Order in the 1940s. The first phase of the work, completed in 1998, accommodates the textile, fine art, sculpture and pottery departments.

The primary concern for the architects was to create a coherent plan whereby each of the separate departments might relate to one another.

Within the existing building large spaces to be used for drawing and fabrication were provided by breaking out walls to the existing cells, while in other areas new skylights were incorporated to introduce north light. The existing internal corridors were brightened up by replacing solid doors with tall glazed doors and punctuated along their length by tall pivot doors.

Students undertake their personal projects in individual cells where these have been retained and their work is stored in purpose-designed mobile stainless-steel drawing chests located in the wide corridors.

On the ground-floor corridor running east–west Portuguese stone and maple wood have been laid to enliven the previously sombre décor. At the eastern corner there is a new library on five floors constructed in oak. From here students have views of Galway Bay. As a counterpoint, a dedicated art house/cinema will be provided at the west end in the second phase of work begun in 1999.

Across the north elevation a new sculpture workshop has been built around an old elm tree. The roof is made up of a number of vaulted corrugated-iron roofs with east-facing clerestorey lighting.

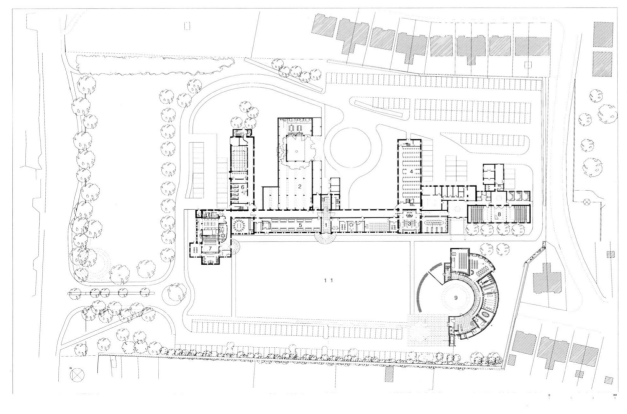

Ground plan:
1. *Entrance Hall*
2. *Sculpture Workshop*
3. *Library*
4. *Studio*
5. *Restaurant*
6. *Film and Video*
7. *Proposed Cinema*
8. *Music*
9. *Future Teacher Centre*
10. *Car park*
11. *Forecourt*

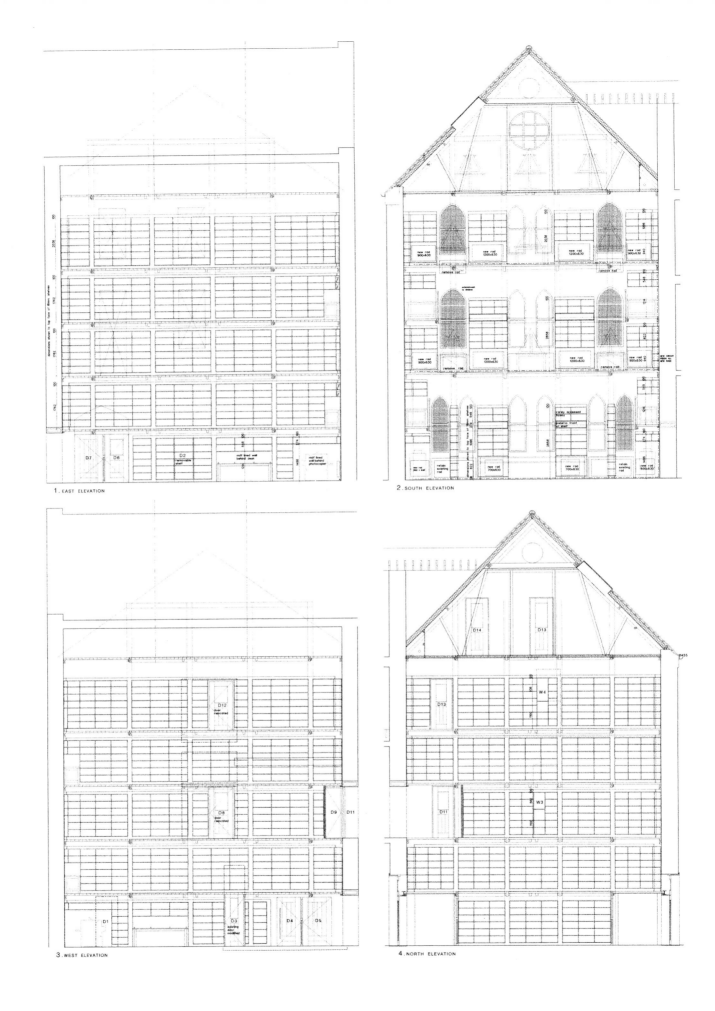

1. EAST ELEVATION

2. SOUTH ELEVATION

3. WEST ELEVATION

4. NORTH ELEVATION

UNIVERSITY OF NANTES SCHOOL OF ECONOMIC SCIENCES AND LAW LIBRARY

Nantes, France

Simplicity and evidence. These are the two principles that have guided how the design of this new project is integrated within the existing university.

The possibility of siting the building within protected woodland and the need to connect the different elements of the university led to the need to finish the campus. However, the building is more than a simple extension – it brings a new contemporary variation, that surpasses the original idea. Looking to l'Erdre, it acts as a filter between campus and woodland and also provides a network of links between the different elements of the university.

The apparent contradiction, that the project is both a grouping of liaising buildings and a point of traffic confluence, is addressed by fragmenting the buildings' volumes, while retaining the view towards l'Erdre from the entrance to the university.

The Ange Guepin Department of Social Science is situated on one side of the plan and the Department of Economic Sciences and the library of the School of Economic Sciences and Law is on the other. These three different functional parts of the campus are brought together to form an harmonious whole, yet are fragmented like the elements of a bar code: the dark strips of the buildings contrast with the lighter strips of the views of woodland, with empty spaces between them. The strips vary in width according to the requirements of the programme. The progressive compactness of the woodland strips from south to north contrasts with the large, parallel building of the Department of Social Science, which stands out rather like a punctuation mark and is a key feature in the project, as well as on the university campus. Compared to all the other buildings on the site which tower at 12 metres, the Department of Social Science reaches its highest point at 18 metres.

The whole bar code system is then split in two by a large diagonal which contains all the entrances and halls of the buildings. This brings together the entire architectural composition by forming a visual link, the edges of which are reinforced by rows of lime trees, from one building to the other.

The bar code is an evolutionary project and over time grow through the extension of the library and the woodland strips, continuing to add to the vitality of the university.

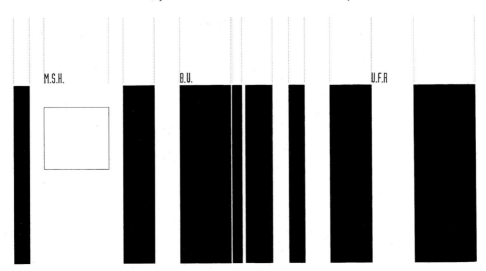

M.S.H. B.U. U.F.R

Site plan

Perspective view

Bird's-eye view

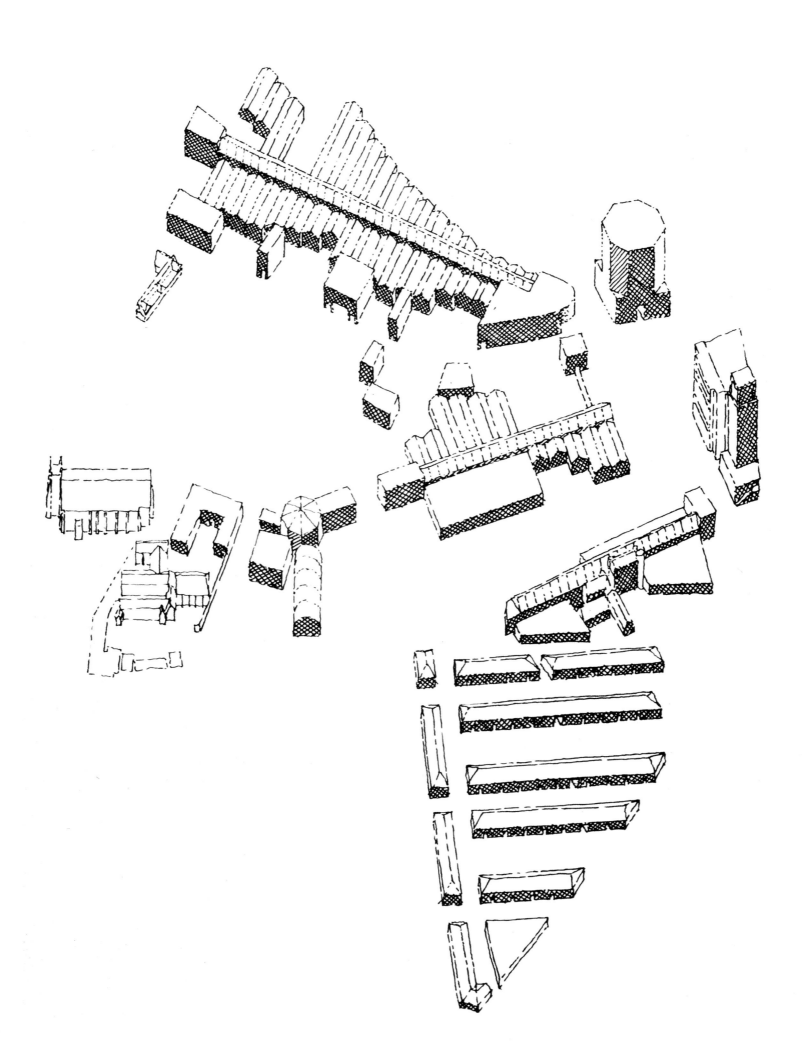

CROYDON UNIVERSITY CAMPUS MASTERPLAN

Croydon, United Kingdom

In 1992, together with other practices, we were invited by the Architectural Foundation to participate in an urban design initiative on Croydon. We were assigned the neglected area of Croydon Old Town. After some deliberation we decided to test the idea of a 'community' university for Croydon and, by extension, to re-examine the more general idea of the mutual interdependency of university and city.

In the 1960s land in the centre of cities was expensive and as a result whole new campuses were built on the peripheries – for example, East Anglia, Bath and Dublin. Experience has shown that in spite of the wish to stimulate an urban environment the campuses have remained barren and instrumental. Thirty years later the position has been reversed. Many essential city functions have been siphoned off into suburbs in the form of business parks and regional shopping centers. 'Edge City' has emerged leaving large sections of centre abandoned and in search of a new role.

Unlike the new universities, the polytechnics have always had a foothold in the center of cities. With their new university status and enlarged enrolment, the ex-polytechnics have an opportunity to redefine and expand essential relationships to the city. Croydon offered such an opportunity. Since its medieval origins the old town had developed organically, up to the 1960s with the dramatic expansion centred on the railway station, but with the introduction of urban motorways in the 1970s it became cut off and was allowed to decay. Croydon became polarised – a city of objects expressed by individual office towers versus the city of continuous fabric expressed by the streets of the old town. There is a clear diagram evident in the map of Croydon. A straight line along the axis of St George Street links the main station to the old town. At right angles to this are bands of contrasting development. First the city of freestanding office buildings, then the commercial city of the high street and, finally, the decaying old town centred on Church Street.

The idea of a community university developed from

Opposite: Site plan

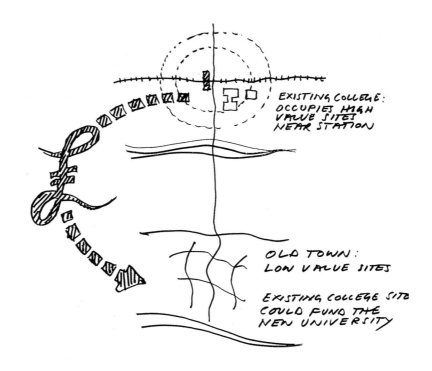

EXISTING COLLEGE: OCCUPIES HIGH VALUE SITES NEAR STATION

OLD TOWN: LOW VALUE SITES

EXISTING COLLEGE SITE COULD FUND THE NEW UNIVERSITY

Conceptual layout drawings

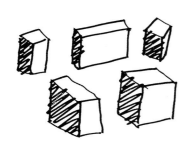

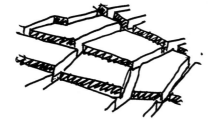

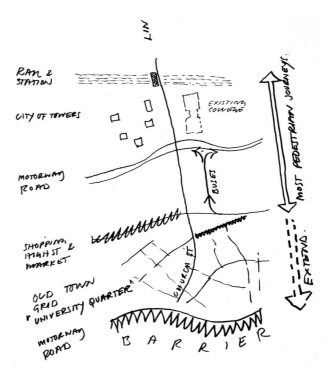

INDIVIDUAL TOWERS – NO LIFE AT GROUND LEVEL – ACTIVITY LOCKED INTO THE BUILDING ENVELOPE

HORIZONTAL GRID – STREET LIFE – MAXIMUM CONTACT BETWEEN DISSIMILAR ACTIVITIES

CROYDON – CITY OF TOWERS   CROYDON – OLD TOWN

A N A L O G Y

POST WAR UNIVERSITIES LOCATED OUTSIDE TOWNS

HISTORIC UNIVERSITIES INTEGRATED INTO TOWNS

the following impulses: first, that Croydon was without a strong cultural base; and, second, that all the ingredients were there to provide one. Croydon College of Higher Education with its 13,000 students and highly regarded fine art and drama schools housed in inadequate and overcrowded accommodation in the commercial centre, provided the hypothetical client. The emphasis on part-time and vocational courses made the college an interesting model for a new interpretation of a commercial university.

Our proposition was to relocate Croydon College into the partly abandoned fabric of the old town, a fabric without much commercial value but geographically close to the centre. Thus we could fully integrate the university into the life of the town. The old town has a clear pattern of streets and public buildings, in contrast to the ambiguous city of freestanding objects in the commercial centre. Within this pattern, however, there are significant voids in the street frontage, leading to extensive and derelict backlands. The organisation of those voids into the strategic routes began to suggest an elementary pattern similar to 19th-century arcades. Within this matrix, each department would have a recognisable street frontage with studios or workshops behind. The School of Catering, for example, might generate a restaurant, the School of Fine Arts a gallery and the School of Drama a theatre, so allowing life in the street and life in the university to overlap.

The architecture of the project is intentionally low-key and resists the emphasis on three-dimensional imagery normally associated with university buildings. The development of the interior of the block employs top-lit inexpensive shed buildings, two to three storeys in height. Not unlike 19th-century artists' studios and arcades they would be mostly interiors built up to the boundaries, with the separating divide of the party wall. This pattern of sheds would be connected by double-height glazed corridors acting as the collective university space. We made two complementary models to express this idea – one out of plaster of Paris whereby the walls to the boundary and the internal routes act as the framework to the continuous build fabric, and the second in cardboard expressing the notional party walls of individual departments.

The accidental is important to the style of the project. Here and there the internal route would bump into, and give new life to, an unlikely group of existing and underused buildings – a fine 15th-century church, a bishop's palace, a waterworks and an abandoned department store. These structures, while maintaining continuity with Croydon Old Town, also provide suitable accommodation for ceremonial and collective university occasions. Added to this, the surrounding streets have a stock of ordinary and underoccupied terraced housing that would serve well as inexpensive student residences. The whole would represent a student quarter fully integrated into urban life. In order to express the relationship of university fabric to the town's public buildings we produced plan drawings of the old town in the convention of Batista Noli's survey of Rome. Here the public interiors of buildings are given the same spatial category as external streets and squares. The resulting figure-ground expresses a more porous and complex relationship between street and urban block, and between the university and the town.

Site plans

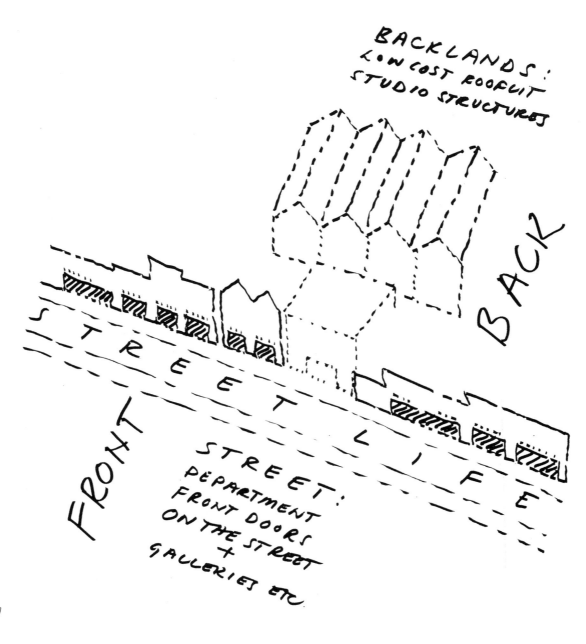

BACKLANDS:
LOW COST ROOFLIT
STUDIO STRUCTURES

BACK

STREET LIFE

FRONT

STREET:
DEPARTMENT
FRONT DOORS
ON THE STREET
+
GALLERIES ETC.

Concept drawing

Site plan

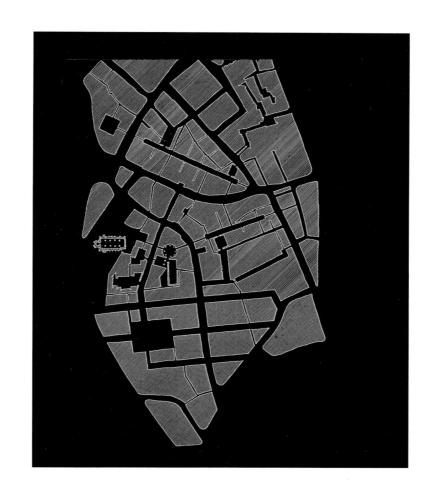

Site plans

JEREMY DIXON, EDWARD JONES ARCHITECTS

UNIVERSITY OF CAMBRIDGE
DARWIN COLLEGE STUDY CENTRE

Cambridge, United Kingdom

The purpose of the building is to provide facilities for postgraduate students to study in a good working atmosphere. The study centre is designed to offer a choice of environments: overlooking the River Cam, sitting outside on the balcony or steps, looking towards Silver Street, sitting around a large table, choosing to be isolated under the lantern, relaxing on a sofa or working in the dedicated computer rooms.

The site, a long narrow rectangle, lies between the curve of Silver Street and the Cam millpool. The college itself is linear in plan. Over time existing buildings were joined together by new connecting buildings. The site is therefore the linear end of a linear plan.

On the street side the building is low and emerges from the existing curved boundary wall. On the river side there are two storeys of accommodation, and within this section computer rooms are placed at ground-floor level along the riverfront. The main reading room is a space that extends from the ground floor to the first floor and overlooks the water. This gives the opportunity to provide a variety of study spaces.

The interior of the building resembles one large piece of furniture. Structure, cladding, windows, floors, bookcases and furniture are all made of oak. The timber has different characteristics varying from the dramatic texture of shakes and splits visible in the structure to the delicate refinement of veneers in the furniture.

The dominant aspect of the interior space comes from the geometry of the roof. The straight line in the plan, generated by the waterside and echoed by the clerestory, is set against the curved wall which leads to Silver Street. The inside of the wall is lined with books and the rafters forming the roof reconcile the straight line to the curve and generate a gentle three-dimensional curved plane when seen in perspective.

The building is constructed of brickwork and English oak with soft lime mortar used to avoid movement in joints. The oak structure uses sections of a size that were only available 'green' or unseasoned. Although the timber was specially cut and dried for the project, the moisture content nevertheless remains in the range of 25 to 60 per cent and the structure will continue to dry for several years. The timber joints which transfer loadbearing between surfaces use a system of stainless-steel mechanical fixings to allow them to be tightened as the timber dries. The oak rafters which form the surface act compositely with a double skin of plywood deck and provide lateral stability. The ground floor is of natural stone and the roofs are of natural slate and lead.

At the head of the plan are a seminar room, a small flat and a timber lantern. To avoid the use of opening windows on the street side, the lantern opens and closes automatically, providing cross-ventilation to the reading areas.

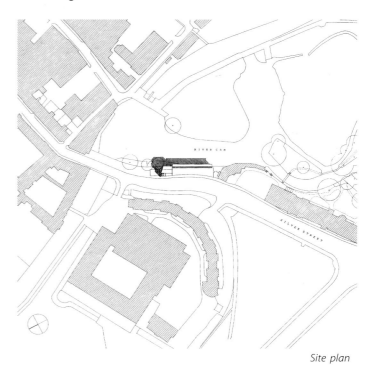

Site plan

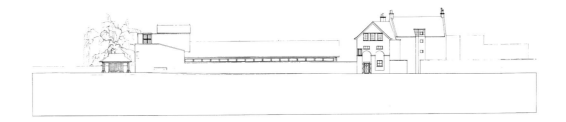

Street elevation

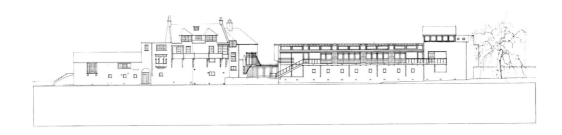

River elevation

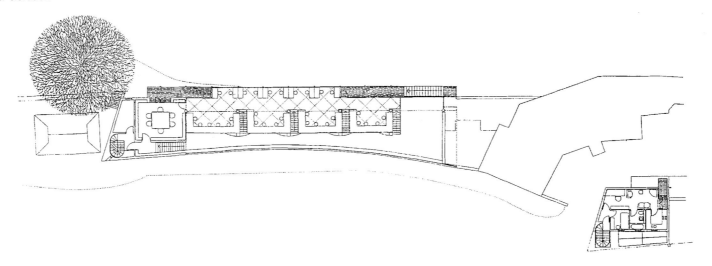

First floor plan

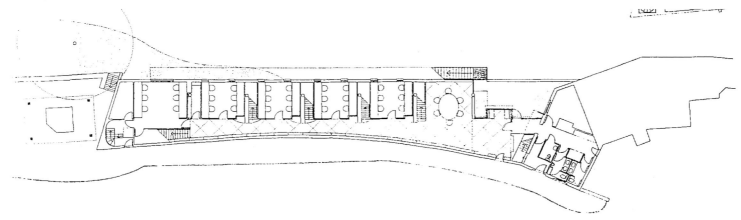

Ground floor plan

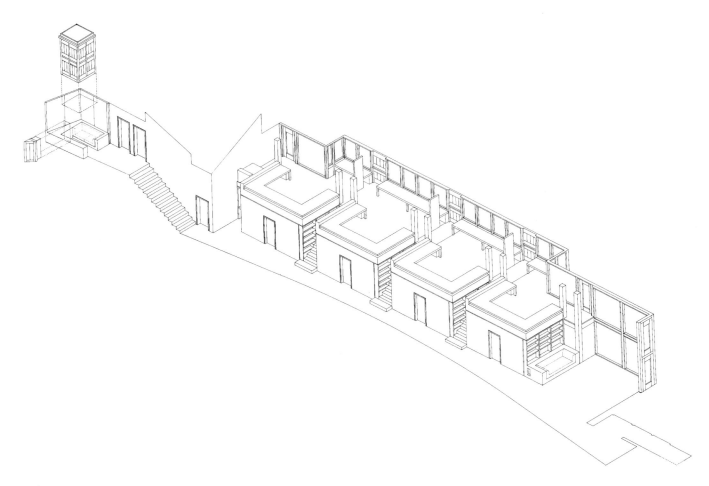

Axonometric

UNIVERSITY OF PORTSMOUTH SCIENCE BUILDING

Portsmouth, United Kingdom

The city of Portsmouth required a building that would provide a suitable landmark to a prominent corner site in its centre. The site is particularly visible when seen in perspective from St Michael's Road. In addition, the building is to anticipate more conventional future development of the White Swan car park to the east. The city further requested that the height of the new building should create a transition between the existing six-storey university building and the future four-storey development on the White Swan site.

The building is also an early contribution to the new masterplan for the University of Portsmouth, prepared by Professor Sir Colin Stansfield Smith, in which the science departments are to be consolidated here and on adjacent sites. To this end it is to provide an extension to the existing St Michael's Building.

Unlike the adjacent freestanding King Henry and St Michael's buildings, the proposed new science building almost totally occupies its irregular site. Also, unlike the equivalent facades of these neighbouring buildings, it provides distinct and different elevations. At the corner facing the intersection at St Michael's Road and King Richard I Street, the curved facade acts as a shield to the noise of traffic and the southerly exposure. Here the windows are set flush in a six-storey facade of silver aluminium panels, while the semicircular corner prow forms the landmark and conceals the exposed flank of the incomplete St Michael's Building. At ground level a pedestrian underpass cuts into the corner and forms a flat panel for the building sign. This closes off the long view afforded motorists as they proceed north along St Michael's Road.

The east elevation facing the city car park expresses the structural frame and is four storeys high. It forms one side of a proposed pedestrian street which gives access to the main entrance. As the St Michael's Building does not have a creditable front door, it is

proposed that this entrance will serve both buildings. Turning the corner into White Swan Road the facade is relatively neutral with windows to the escape stairs. It is here that the lift lobbies and connections to St Michael's are positioned, with natural light and views to the United Services playing fields to the southwest.

The building provides accommodation for the pharmacy, physics and research departments. With the exception of the lecture theatres and the large teaching laboratories, which are accommodated in the semicircular corner (20 metres in diameter), the remaining accommodation is planned in a less specific and more flexible manner.

In contrast to the relatively neutral colours of the exterior (silver, grey and black) the interiors are animated by a strong polychromy. The palette of colours is restricted to public areas of the building, to lecture theatres and to areas of general circulation. These combine to contrast with the laboratories and research rooms which the client requested should be painted white throughout.

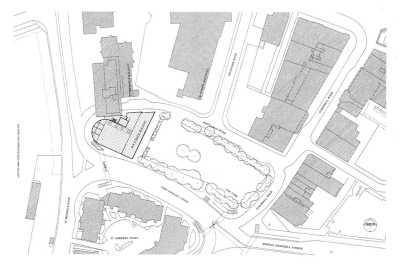

Site plan

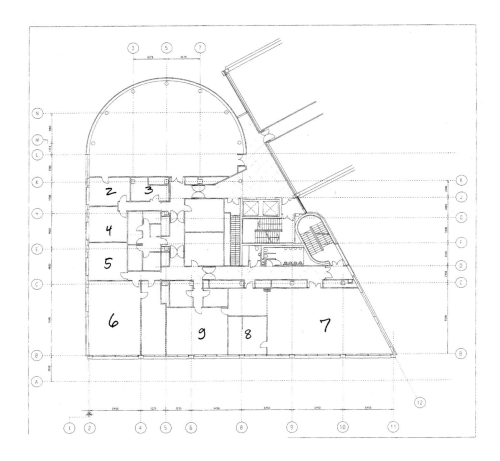

First floor plan

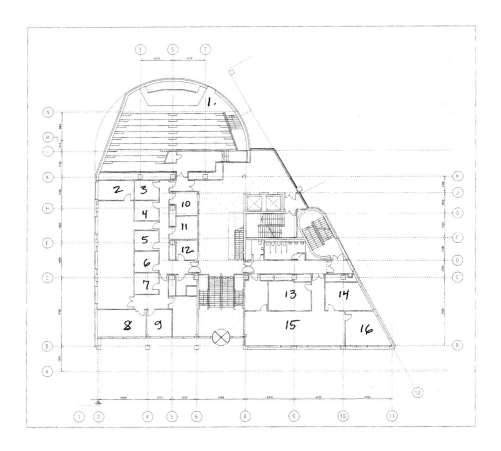

Ground floor plan

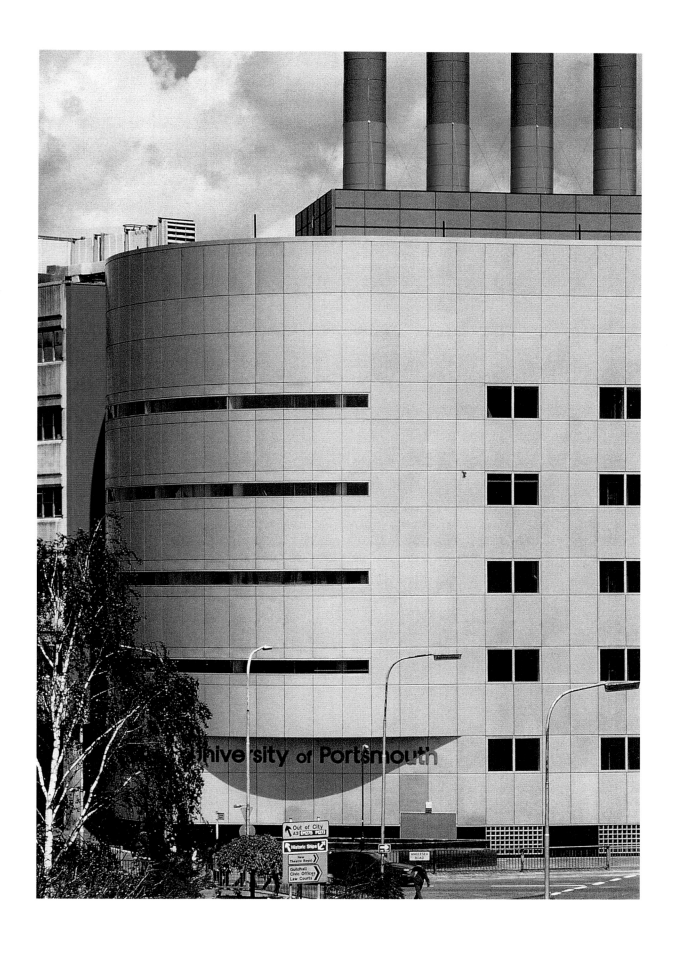

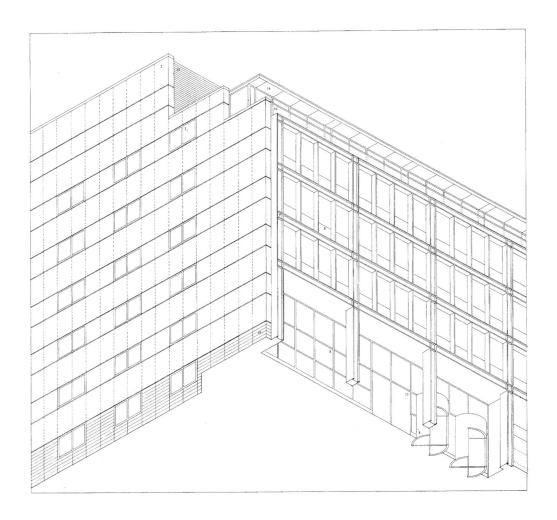

Isometric

LYCÉE ALBERT CAMUS

Fréjus, France

Fréjus is a rapidly expanding town on the Côte d'Azur in southern France. The need for a Lycée Polyvalent was identified in response to the increasing population in the area. The lycée provides places for 900 students and comprises specialised teaching spaces as well as traditional classrooms.

The site straddles a hill with fine views out towards the sea and hills. The building is linear in form, two storeys high and maximises the fine views to the south. The internal arrangement establishes a street with all classrooms opening off it so that it is the social focus for the lycée. Externally, the building is rooted in the landscape by the use of tree planting, with the tree forms echoing the sweep of the roof.

The method of ventilating the building in the hot climate relies on techniques familiar from traditional Arab architecture. This led to the use of a concrete structure to provide thermal mass in order to absorb temperature variations, as well as to the choice of a building form that would enhance natural ventilation using a stack effect, thus avoiding the need to ventilate the building mechanically: the lofty internal street creates a solar chimney to induce the flow of air. Traditional features such as *brise soleil* are also used to shade the south elevation.

The requirement for rapid construction was met by adopting a simple repetitive concrete frame which permitted the sequences of construction to follow in logical phases, one after another, to maximise efficiency. Work began on site in September 1992 and was completed in August 1993: the construction programme required the completion of the 243 metre long, 14,500m^2 building in less than 12 months. By taking maximum advantage of repetition, not only were construction costs reduced, but construction time was also minimised. The building was completed within the client's budget: the final construction cost

was 80 million francs, 5 million francs below the original budget framework.

The materials for the building were chosen to respond to local construction techniques and climate. The exposed concrete structure makes use of the French tradition of good quality *in situ* concrete. A metal-faced framework and a specially prepared concrete mix were used to ensure a high standard of finish.

Planning the building with a long central street gave the opportunity for the structure to combine economy with elegance and speed of construction, despite being located in an earthquake region. Through the economies of repetition, it allowed a series of modular structural units enveloping the different internal spaces to be designed at a construction cost comparable to that for smaller-span structures. Each unit contains a vaulted concrete roof shell, which uses the full depth of the vault to span directly on to columns. The first floor is a regular concrete ribbed slab, and columns are located only along the street and the external elevations.

The use of concrete gives a high thermal mass and radiant cooling to the building, both of which are significant contributions to the structure's low-energy principles. Repetition of the modules allowed many uses to be obtained from a high quality framework, producing excellent concrete finishes at an economic cost.

The double-storey-height circulation space along the street between the classroom blocks provides ventilation and allows daylight to reach the internal facades. The street canopy has ventilation louvres, which are controlled to ensure ventilation air is drawn from the street by the heating effect of the sun on the canopy (thermosyphon effect) or by wind action.

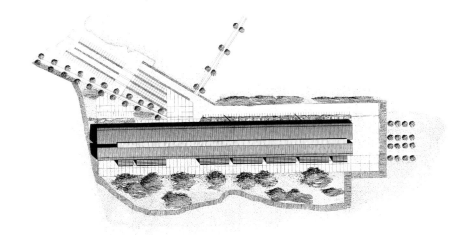

Site plan

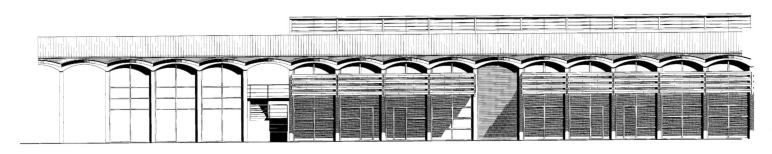

Elevation

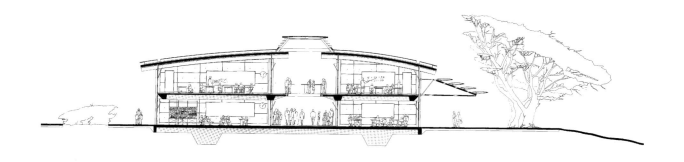

Section

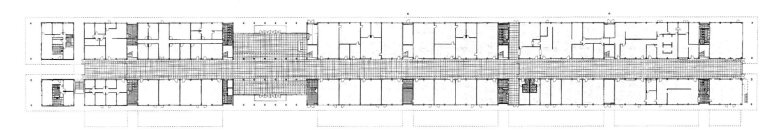

Floor plan

The classrooms are arranged on either side of the street with large adjustable opening lights on the internal and external facades to provide controllable natural ventilation throughout the year. The high ceilings allow unwanted heat gains to stratify, the heated air rising to a high level, away from the occupied space, where it may be removed by ventilation. A metal outer roof is provided over the well-insulated concrete roof and the air space between is ventilated to reduce solar gains reaching the interior via the roof.

Mechanical ventilation is provided only where dictated by the room function, for example, in kitchens and laboratories. Where required by the client specification, air conditioning has been provided within the hotel and catering areas. Heating for the building is provided by a conventional radiator system with gas-fired boiler plant. The major services distribution is via the undercroft and service cores; the final services distribution is generally concealed in the floor and roof structures.

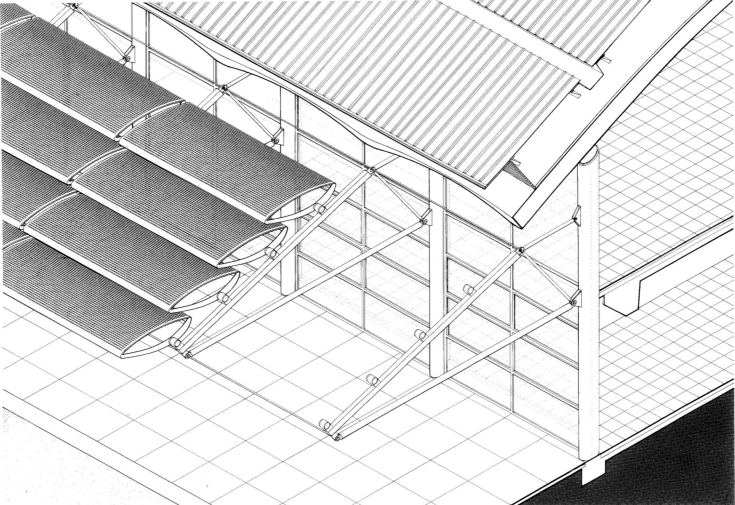

Drawing of
sun shading

ROBERT GORDON UNIVERSITY FACULTY OF MANAGEMENT

Aberdeen, United Kingdom

The opening of Robert Gordon University's Faculty of Management marks the completion of the first stage of the 20-year plan to relocate most of the university, currently housed in eight separate teaching sites, to a greenfield site on the north bank of the River Dee. Foster and Partners is responsible for both the masterplan and the design of the first new faculty building.

The masterplan creates a linear pedestrian street which connects the proposed faculty buildings. The site is divided into three zones: car parking to the north, a central zone for buildings and parkland and wildlife to the south. The position of the proposed faculty buildings corresponds to the old agricultural pattern of the east–west linear sequence of fields separated by hedgerows. The masterplan will strengthen existing tree lines and enhance the micro-climate to benefit both the site and the people living on it.

The dramatic sweeping profile of the new faculty is a response to the rolling topography of the land and the existing tree canopy. The intention was to have as little impact as possible on the surrounding areas of woodland, which shelter the site and conceal the development from the road. The building has a concrete frame which terraces down the natural slope of the site. The terraces are oversailed by a light curved roof, constructed of steel beams supported on slender steel columns with a lightweight self-finished aluminium deck. The roof beams project beyond the building envelope and terminate in the landscape. Granite cladding panels alternating with infill panels of aluminium and glass emphasise the structural from that of the concrete frame. New Kemnay granite, the traditional granite used in the architecture of

Aberdeen, was chosen to clad the building.

The university's accommodation is arranged on either side of a central street. Where the street passes through the heart of the building, a four-storey-high atrium is created, naturally lit from above via glazed rooflights which occupy the full width of the building. All teaching, library and office areas are accessed from this street, office and catering space to the north and teaching and library space to the south. A secondary linear atrium runs perpendicular to the street and together they provide the faculty with, most importantly, an informal meeting place which encourages interaction between students and staff. They also provide entry and security for the building and a corridor for access to teaching areas. The two main access points into the street are expressed by a recessed four-storey-high glazed wall. Internal glazing provides soundproofing for the staff space and library. Spaces for student common rooms are located at the southern end of the building overlooking a winter garden, which in turn opens out on to the shaded external terraces by the river.

Low maintenance, high quality finishes were chosen throughout to ensure durability and low maintenance costs. A concept of protective dados was developed for heavily used areas such as the corridors in basement areas which have walls of fair-faced blockwork. Classrooms have blockwork to a level of 1 metre above the finished floor to provide protection where it is most needed. Similarly, maple panels are used in the library and balustrades are made of glass with handrails of stainless steel. These low maintenance solutions were arrived at through the close cooperation of the university's staff with the design team.

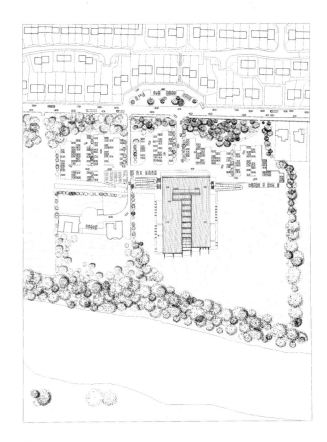

Site plan

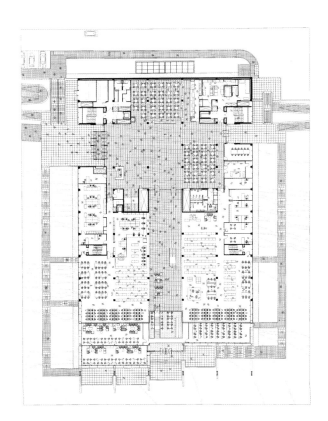

Floor plan

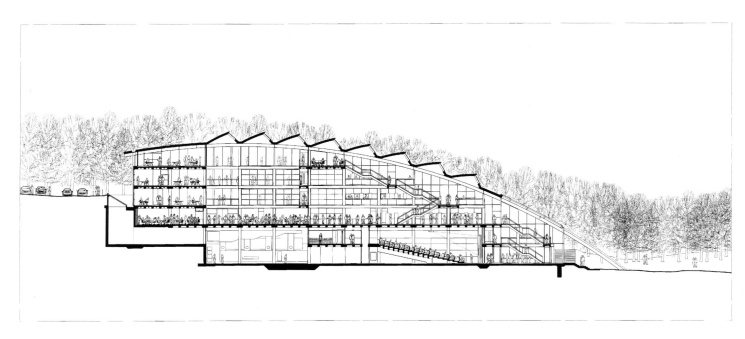

Section

UNIVERSITY OF CAMBRIDGE FACULTY OF LAW

Cambridge, United Kingdom

The aim of the architects has been to preserve the enviable context of this building, while providing the Faculty of Law with a new focus. It includes the Squire Law Library, five new auditoria, seminar rooms, and common rooms and administrative offices and is close to the Institute of Criminology, the university library and principal arts faculty buildings. The new building is expressive of the university's desire to provide the most up-to-date facilities for teaching and research.

Four storeys high – with a further two floors below ground level – the new building does not intrude into the established skyline. However, it has a gravitas appropriate to its function, achieved by the use of durable and beautiful modern materials, in particular natural stone. The single rectangular platform is dramatically terminated with a diagonal cut to respond both to the form of the history faculty and to the fine trees on the lawn in front.

Natural light is used to dramatic effect, especially in the library which occupies the top three floors, where benefit is taken of the fully glazed north-facing elevation. Working areas are designed to have views out over the gardens.

The ground floor contains administrative offices and studies for staff. The lower ground floors are taken up by auditoria, book stores and the student common room, and are lit naturally by means of a full-height atrium and structural glass floors on the north edge.

The interior is a luminous and highly efficient space, unified in theme but carefully considered in terms of the range of activities it houses.

The concrete floors are enclosed above ground by a triangulated steel Vierendeel structure, cylindrical in section, to which the cladding systems are fixed. this triangular format allows the repetitive use of single glazed panel size and has been developed with YRM Anthony Hunt Associates to maximise structural efficiency.

Externally, the curved layout of the north facade's structural silicon glazing develops into a stainless-steel roof above. The east and west facades are also finished with glass which is treated to combat solar heat gain and glare. The west wall forms a sinusoidal curve in plan – a function of the triangular steelwork geometry. The vertical south facade is clad in reconstituted Portland stone reflecting the solid form of the existing raised faculty building opposite, while the law faculty offices are clad with translucent glazing with clear horizontal vision strips which also incorporate opening windows to provide natural ventilation.

The law faculty building demonstrates the practice's strong interest in education, and embodies the architects' concern to create humane modern buildings that respond positively both to their surroundings and the needs of an energy-conscious client.

Site plan

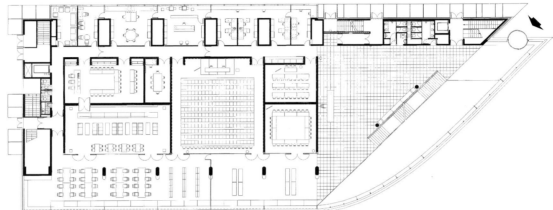

Second floor plan

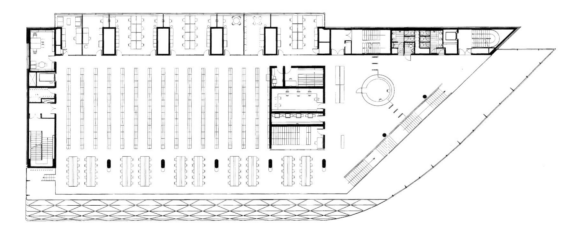

Ground floor plan

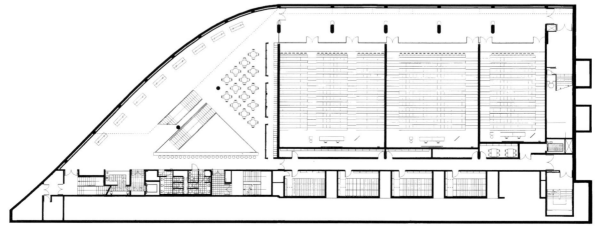

Lower floor plan

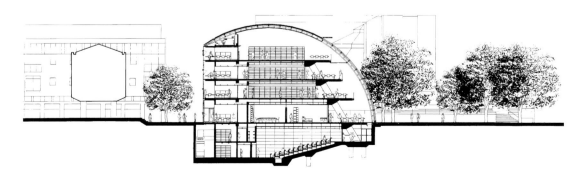

Section

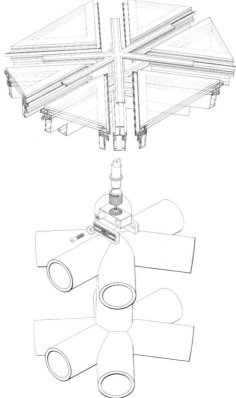

Structural diagram

SAINT-LEU UNIVERSITY FACULTY OF SCIENCES
Amiens, France

The university buildings have been integrated with the canal system of Amiens and their design has been influenced by their proximity to the city; the university extension is carefully related to the scale of the surrounding houses. A footbridge spans the Canal des Minimes, providing access to the corner of rue Edmond Fontaine and rue des Archers.

The entrance articulates the ground plan. It is directly connected to the three major components of the programme: the teaching departments; the practical activities building; and the research departments. The main building material is brick, which is traditional in Amiens.

The teaching departments are situated immediately off the vast entrance hall and run along the rue des Archers, alongside which a canal has been built linking three other existing canals in a loop. Three lecture halls adjoin the hall. The largest is situated on the ground floor and the other two are on the upper floor and look on to the hall through a mezzanine level which is also accessible via ramps. Moving from the entrance, a gallery provides access to all theoretical courses via a bridge structure. The gallery is directly connected to the lecture halls. The language laboratories, which stand on piles so that they can be clearly seen from the entrance to the garden, are linked to the theoretical departments and the practical departments on the first floor.

The departments for practical activities are acces-sible from the mezzanine in the hall area and are housed in a wing that runs parallel to the teaching departments. The two arms formed by this and the teaching departments flank a large garden in the axis of the composition they form with the entrance hall. There is a small courtyard between the hall and the language laboratory wing through which the Canal des Minimes flows.

The building that houses the zoology collection is situated on the canal near the hall; it adjoins the gardens, the courtyard and a third garden in which the store for dangerous research materials is located.

The research building, which is also accessible from the entrance hall, runs right along the 'peninsula' as far as rue Saint-Leu. The biology, physics and chemistry departments are located, in that order, between the entrance hall and rue Saint-Leu. Each department has its own staircase which provides access from the landscaped avenue along the Canal des Minimes.

In the axis of the composition formed by the entrance hall and the two teaching wings, a large asphalted squared, extended by a landscaped garden, is flanked by three halls of residence; these are accessible from rue des Clairons and will be built in the second phase.

This is a complex in which courtyards, passages, gardens and walkways play an important role. They are the means by which the building breathes.

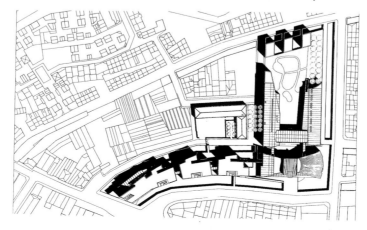

Site plan

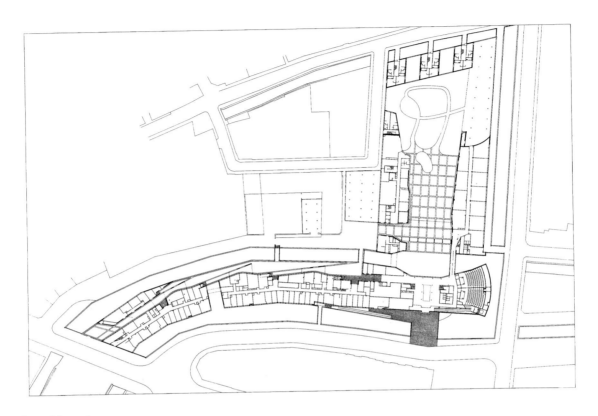

Ground floor plan

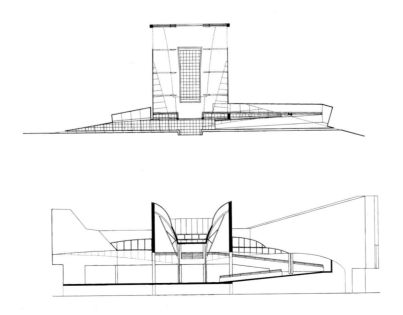

Elevations

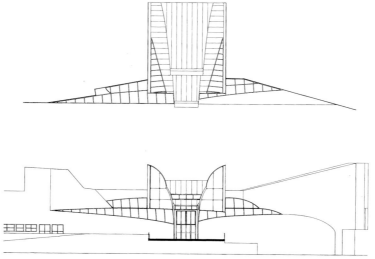

TRINITY COLLEGE DEPARTMENT OF MECHANICAL ENGINEERING

Dublin, Ireland

This project consists of an extension to the 19th-century Parsons Building situated at the southeastern corner of Trinity College campus. It accommodates highly serviced laboratories and workshops, with ancillary seminar rooms and offices. The brief was complex, in terms of specific conditions required for each of the individual workspaces.

The site on this historic campus is sensitive in that it is directly visible from the main body of the campus, and the project involved making a connection to the existing building. While the main geometry of the campus is orthogonal, the granite Parsons Building sat alone, elevated, at an angle to its surroundings. The intention of this scheme was to acknowledge the history and local geometries of the site, resolve the functional requirements and allow the department to have a formal presence on the campus.

The scheme creates a heavy stone base which houses the bulk of the workshops and the engineering laboratories. The base is clad in robust Wicklow granite, with sand and cement pointing. Linear windows cut into this granite base have a double layer in order to abstract and integrate them into the skin. The roof of this space forms a podium and forecourt to Parsons Building. Rooflights in the podium illuminate the workshops below and react to the rhythm of the windows in the original building. A cube element floats above the podium and houses the fluids and acoustic engineering laboratory. This space is roof-lit and has south-facing slit windows and a corner eye. The alignment of the cube links into the formal geometry of the main campus. The cube is clad in a dark, reflective basalt lava which is open jointed. The material was chosen to give expression to the gritty nature of the brief.

Two existing mature lime trees are retained, forming an essential part of the landscape character of the project. Amphitheatre-type steps, together with a sloping grass sward, connect with the trees. The raised cube, Parsons Building and the two lime trees now form part of a new enclosure. These three elements – the new, the old and the organic – create a new place within the walls of the university. The status of the original front door to Parsons Building is reinforced, and is now accessed by means of a grand stepped ramp which replaces the old steps to the building.

A taller element – the book end – finished in a highly polished pigmented plaster, mediates between the scale of the dental hospital to one side and the smaller scale buildings at the western end of the site. It houses the seminar rooms and its tall, sliding metal door and lifting beam allow for deliveries to the ground- and upper-floor laboratories.

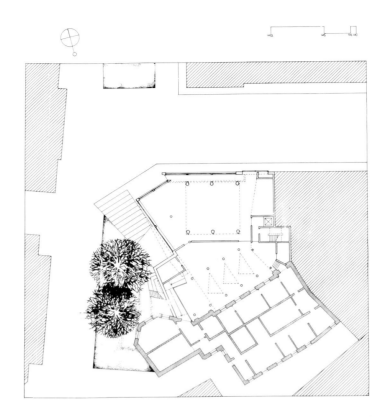

First floor plan

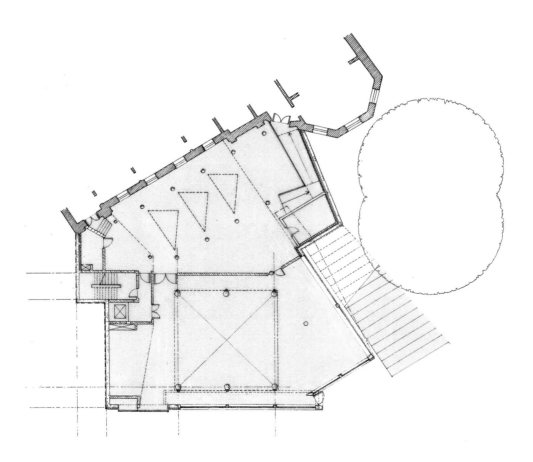

Ground floor plan

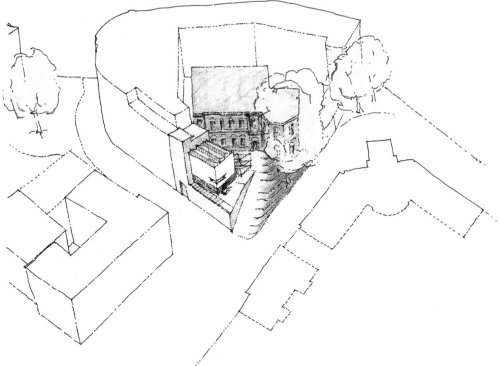

Perspective sketch

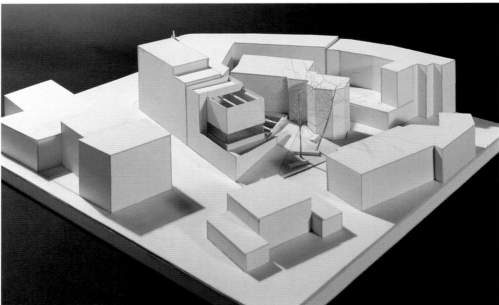

Model

HACKNEY COMMUNITY COLLEGE

London, United Kingdom

The campus comprises more than 27,000m² of college accommodation situated on the redundant 7-acre site of the former Shoreditch Secondary School.

Two major landscaped courtyards form the heart of the campus and highlight the retained trees and Edwardian buildings. The northern courtyard is a large formal space bounded at ground level by the college's administration and commercial facilities. It contains the learning resource centre at a semibasement level, along with a sunken water feature and an amphitheatre which is available for outdoor performances. In contrast the southern courtyard is predominantly soft-landscaped and is virtually surrounded by teaching accommodation. Other small courtyards are incorporated along the Hoxton and Falkirk street frontages.

The two main courtyards are bounded by perimeter colonnades which define major circulation routes and give access to entrances, staircases and lifts. The predominantly hardwood structure accommodates high-level sun louvres that provide shading to the building and will also support lightweight membrane canopies at a low level to offer shelter.

Most of the teaching facilities are housed in linked three-storey blocks constructed in a standardised building form which is intended to be flexible in use and easily adaptable to future change. The links between blocks are formed by vertical service cores and containing entrances, staircases and lifts, lavatories and plant rooms, which constitute the highly serviced and fixed components of the scheme. In contrast the teaching facilities are comprised of flexible shells fitted out with lightweight partitions and finishes that can be altered with the minimum of disruption and cost. By concentrating core and shell facilities, a clear servicing strategy is established and the teaching blocks are free of fixed elements which might inhibit flexibility.

The forms and materials of the buildings have been

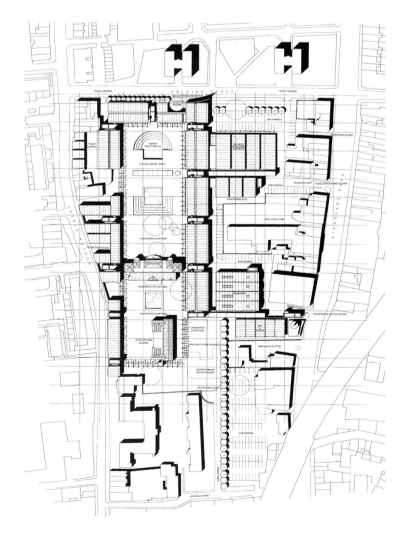

Site plan

Kingsland Road elevation

Long section elevation through courtyards

Typical courtyard bay elevation

Typical section through Teaching Block

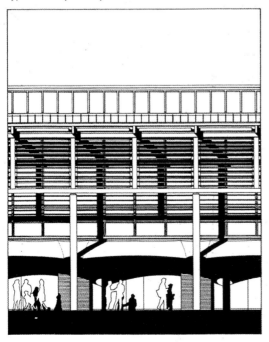

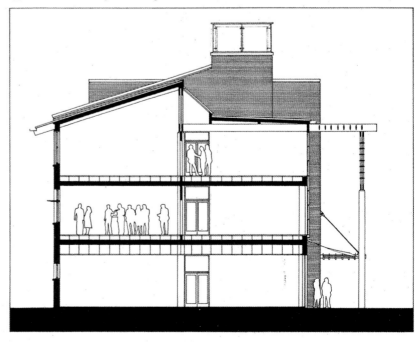

selected to provide cost-effective solutions suited to the college's functions, flexibility in planning and ease of construction. The resulting buildings are mostly concrete-framed structures with masonry external walls and non-loadbearing internal partitions. Where feasible, the design incorporates natural ventilation, daylighting and passive systems to reduce energy and maintenance demands. At a technical level, the design of the new buildings was driven by a desire for future flexibility, energy efficiency and maintenance requirements combined with the constraints of cost and time. Thus the design concept of standardised three-storey blocks lined by vertical service cores was well suited to a phased construction process based on separate but overlapping shell and core fit-out works.

The blocks are of an *in situ* concrete-frame structure.

Tableformwork was used to provide flat floor-slab construction, with each floor constructed off the one below. The blocks have pitched roofs that incorporate glue-laminated timber beams and long-span metal roof construction. The buildings are clad in brickwork with high performance aluminium glazing.

The buildings are highly insulated and the large thermal mass of masonry and concrete is designed to reduce summer cooling loads. Ventilation is generally by natural means via opening windows and rooflights. Heating is by hot water radiators serviced from local gas-fired boilers situated in the roof-level plant rooms within the cores. Heating, security and other services can be controlled centrally via building-management systems.

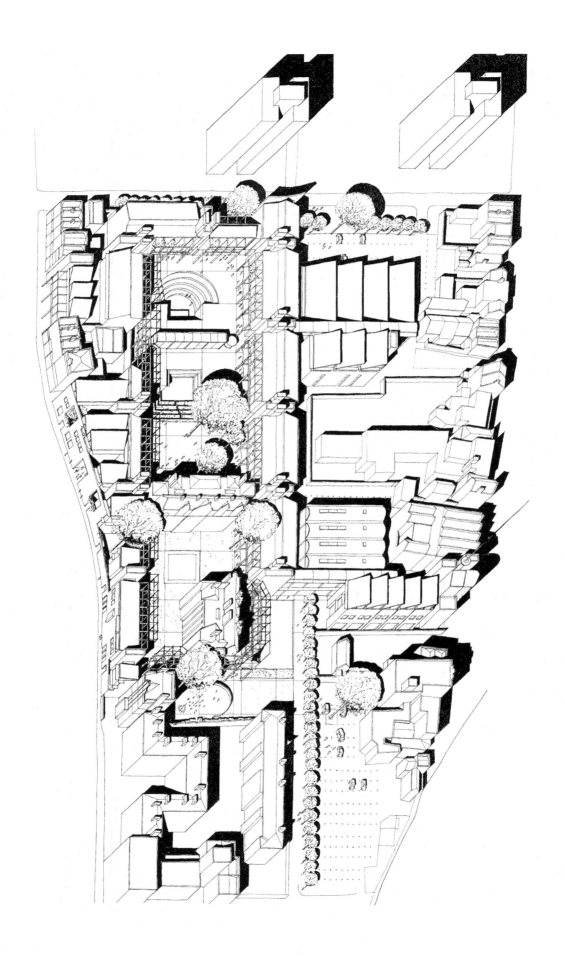

Axonometric

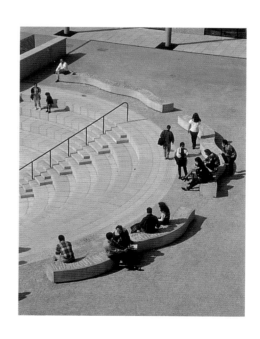

UNIVERSITY OF PORTSMOUTH PORTLAND STREET BUILDING

Portsmouth, United Kingdom

Portsmouth University's new Portland Street Building for its Faculty of Environmental Studies provides a new home for the School of Architecture, Department of Land Construction Management and faculty offices. The planning concept is one of providing an enclosed sanctuary which offers flexibility, security and privacy for students and which is conducive to an effective learning environment.

The design solution is an innovative response to the developed brief and offers a flexible and effective medium to suit the dynamic character of this educational establishment. Aesthetically, the numerous nautical metaphors reflect the important maritime history of the historic city of Portsmouth. The palette of materials is a gradation from the tough, reflective external render, which offers a durable defence to the rigours of a maritime climate, through to the warmth and fineness of selected timber and carpet finishes that is associated with the more intimate spaces within the sanctuary. The structure is conceived as a laboratory of building and environmental experience, and is intended to demonstrate to the building's users the highest standards of building management, accessibility, comfort, durability and flexibility, all achieved with economy in mind.

The tower structures distributed throughout the plan are multifunctional. Their strategic siting offers good accessibility and vertical circulation throughout the building, as well as providing major cores of structural stability. The towers also act as localised energy centres, providing space for plant and rationalised distribution channels for key services. In addition, the circulation and services network offers optimum flexibility for building use and facilitates potential zoning to meet a variety of user demands, as well as minimising constraints on future developments.

The building seeks to maximise the prevailing natural climatic conditions to support a largely passive energy strategy. There is a reliance on the controlled penetration of the sun's rays to provide natural light and solar gains, which are modified by the provision of a reflective and high-thermal-mass structure, perforated with opening windows to enhance natural ventilation. The windows are fitted with a variety of control facilities to counteract excessive gains and glare, while providing a further opportunity for students to control and adjust their environment to the desired level of comfort.

The building form comprises a four-storey U-shaped structure which houses the main teaching and support facilities including studios, a multimedia suite and seminar and tutorial rooms, as well as information technology centres, small lecture spaces and administration accommodation. The U-shaped form encompasses a three-storey nucleus which contains the major lecture facility, review spaces and student social areas. The structures are linked above ground level by strategically positioned bridges. The 6,300m^2 building offers a rich mix of accommodation for the occupying departments and for the faculty and university as a whole. The centre atrium, or forum space, operates as a generous circulation hub and is linked to the encircling accommodation physically and visually through doors and glazed partitions. In addition, the forum space operates as a pivotal teaching space in its own right, where group discussions, conferences and exhibitions of work can be staged; and helps to foster the interactive community of scholars, and stimulate the exchange of ideas that are essential elements of university education. The strategic location of access

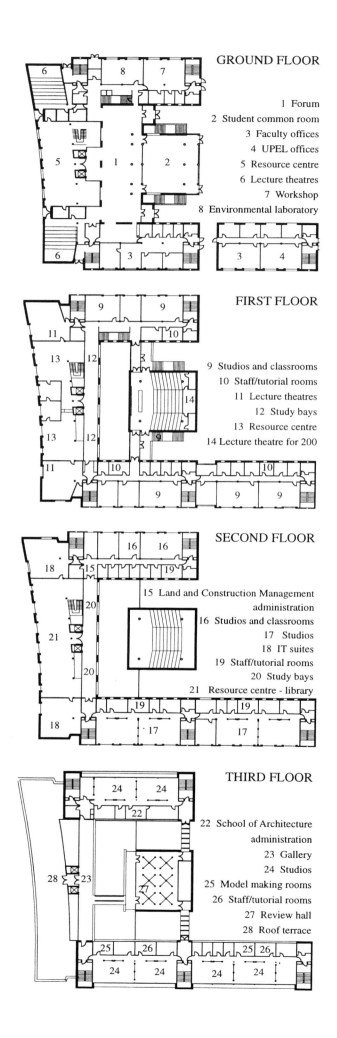

GROUND FLOOR

1 Forum
2 Student common room
3 Faculty offices
4 UPEL offices
5 Resource centre
6 Lecture theatres
7 Workshop
8 Environmental laboratory

FIRST FLOOR

9 Studios and classrooms
10 Staff/tutorial rooms
11 Lecture theatres
12 Study bays
13 Resource centre
14 Lecture theatre for 200

SECOND FLOOR

15 Land and Construction Management
administration
16 Studios and classrooms
17 Studios
18 IT suites
19 Staff/tutorial rooms
20 Study bays
21 Resource centre - library

THIRD FLOOR

22 School of Architecture
administration
23 Gallery
24 Studios
25 Model making rooms
26 Staff/tutorial rooms
27 Review hall
28 Roof terrace

points and vertical circulation shafts within the five service towers offers potential zoning of access to give maximum flexibility in patterns of use.

The design and selection of the construction method and material is a balanced response to the requirements of aesthetic appeal and durability. The main superstructure, which comprises the first three storeys, is of dense masonry construction with applied internal and external rendered finishes. The fourth floor is dominated by a glue-laminated timber structure compromising timber columns and tensegrity trusses which are infilled with glazed screens, both internally and externally, to define the form of accommodation. The entire structure is covered by an insulated, composite, profiled aluminium construction with selected glazed sections to provide ample light and ventilation to the four-storey-high forum space at the heart of the building.

UNIVERSITY OF MANCHESTER CAREER SERVICES UNIT

Manchester, United Kingdom

This office building is to the eastern edge of the University of Manchester campus and is characterised by a 'pavilion' construction which stands in space rather than defining it. It seeks to 'stitch' together the abrupt ends of the adjoining buildings and define a collegiate courtyard.

A wall of polished concrete panels defines the two edges of the site and completes the courtyard on which the layered and rendered building sits. Two folded planar roofs envelop the layers and intersect to generate a dynamic reception/entrance hall which rises through three storeys. This space represents the public face of the careers services unit and contains shared accommodation. Link bridges bisect the space and join the office accommodation housed within the concrete-framed flexible wings. Service accommodation is articulated at the ends of the wings, underpinning this flexibility.

The coffers to the floors are expressed not only to offer a rhythm resonant with the external wall, but also as part of the environmental strategy. This is a naturally ventilated building; extremes in temperature are tempered by the thermal mass and the offices cross-venting into the entrance hall.

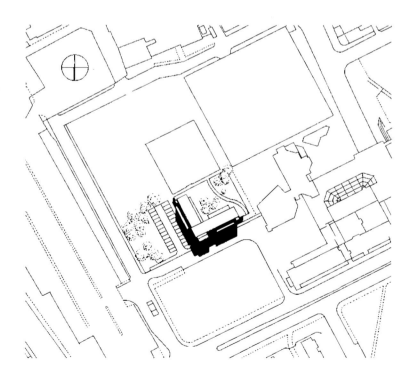

Site plan

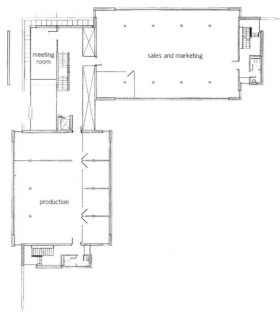

Second floor plan

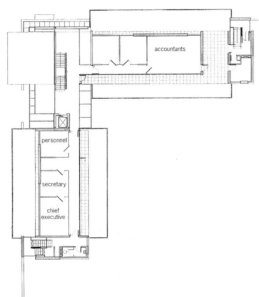

First floor plan

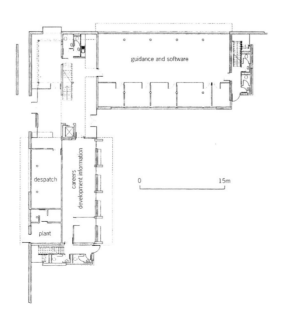

Ground floor plan

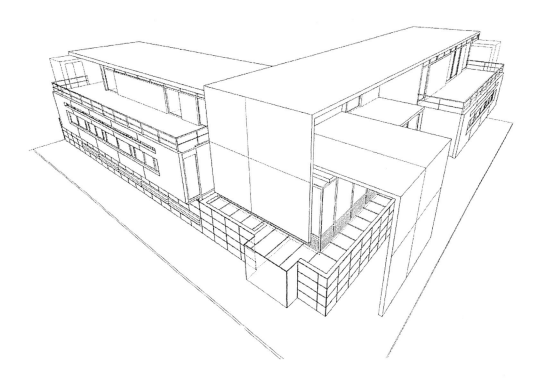

Perspective drawing

UNIVERSITY OF SALFORD CENTENARY BUILDING

Salford, United Kingdom

The building, a four-storey orthogonal structure with a three-storey, highly glazed freeform element facing the courtyard, is of crosswall construction. A series of flat roofs step down from east to west. It provides three significantly different types of accommodation for three departments: cellular rooms for tutors extend the full length of the front of the building; a slightly wider span behind provides space for both flexible studios and seminar rooms; and the wider span of the freeform structure accommodates more flexible CAD suites, lecture theatres and a huge top floor which houses an industrial design studio.

Materials respond to the different uses within the building: the east elevation has a base of rendered blockwork panels, above which is a rainscreen system of Uginox G3 stainless steel; most of the west-facing elevation is steel curtain walling.

Between these elevations there is a linear atrium or street. All horizontal circulation is via galleries overlooking this space, and on the first floor it is possible to cross the atrium void. In this way, street life becomes an aspect of the life of the building; common areas exist within the street in a deliberate attempt to bring about the fusion of the three different departments within their new building. A series of openings within glazed screens provides natural ventilation and brings light into the heart of the building. Glazed north and south ends offer aspects towards Manchester and over the Salford plain. The west elevation is also highly glazed, with an array of *brise soleils*.

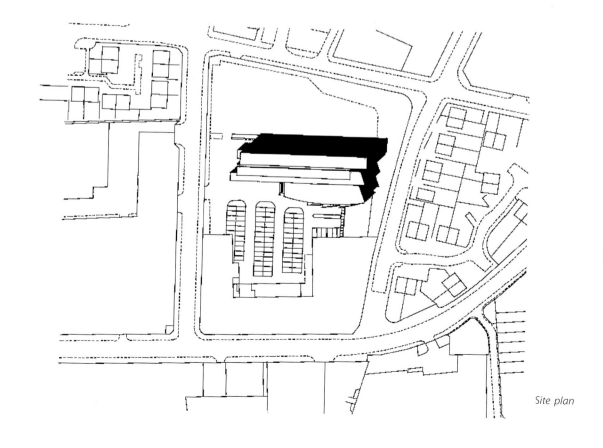

Site plan

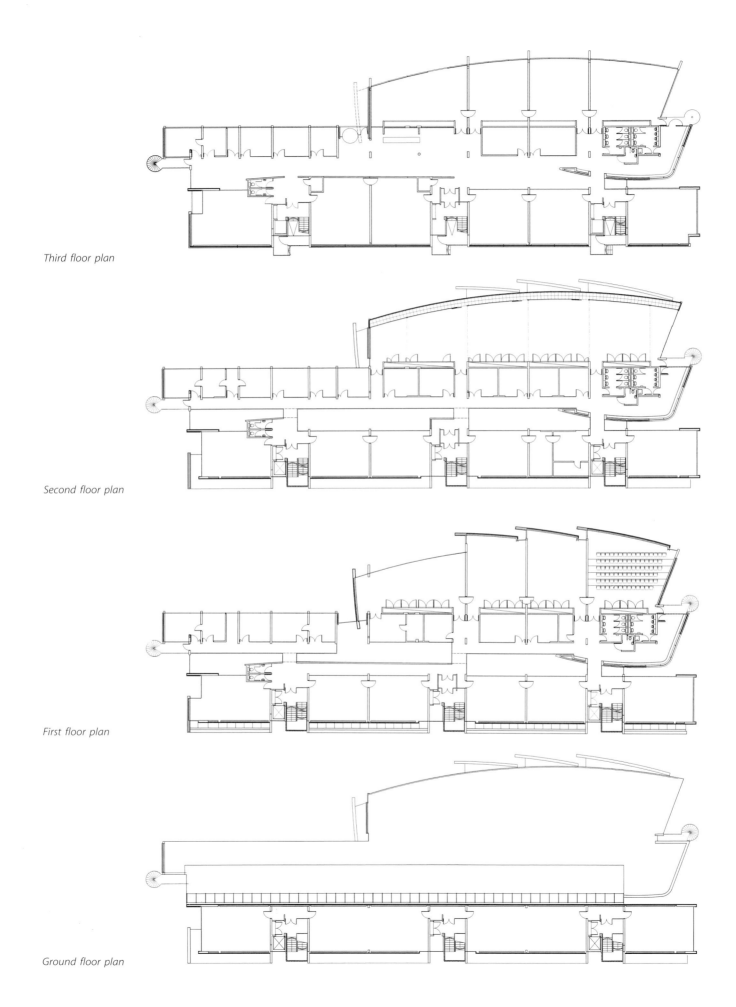

Third floor plan

Second floor plan

First floor plan

Ground floor plan

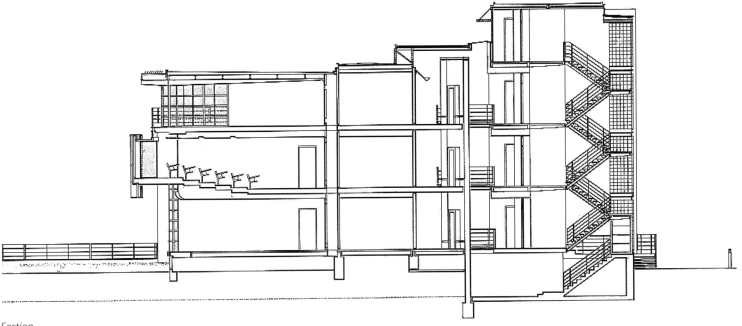

Section

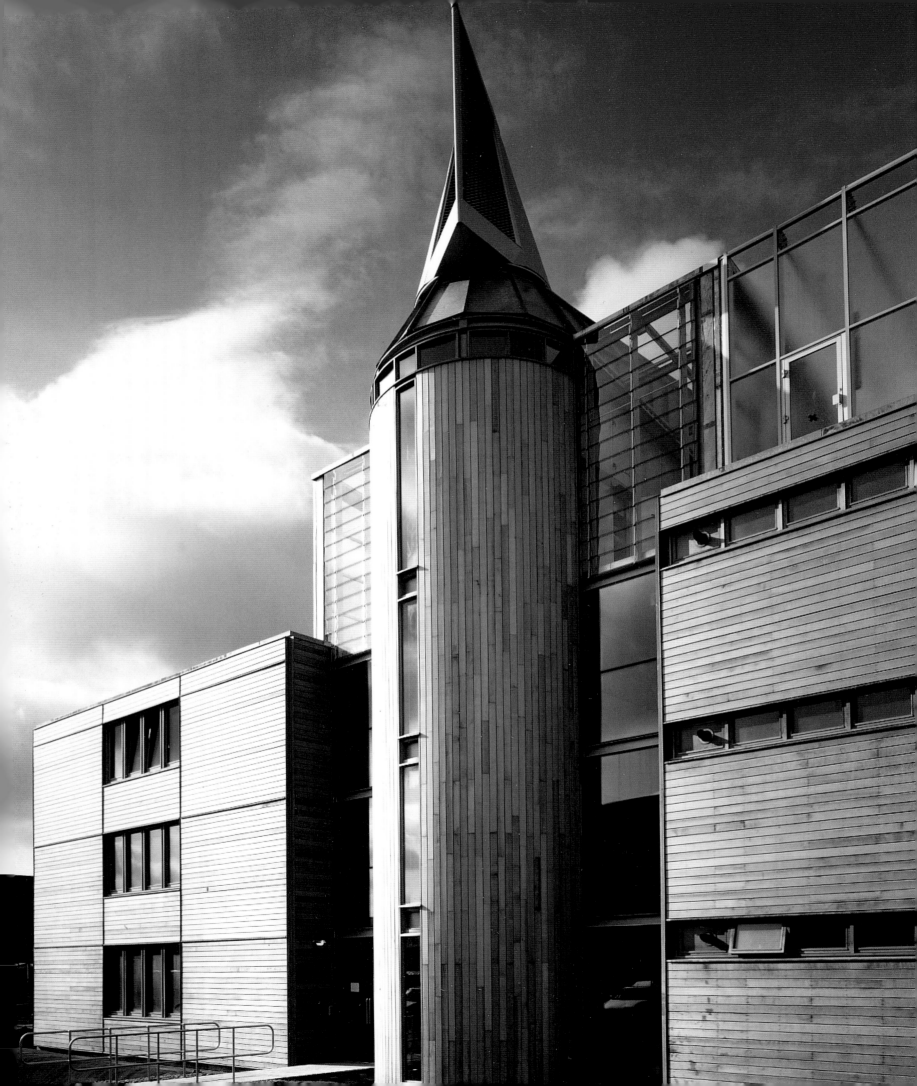

UNIVERSITY OF NOTTINGHAM JUBILEE CAMPUS

Nottingham, United Kingdom

The university's Jubilee Campus turns a former bicycle-factory site into an academic park for 2,500 students, and introduces an energy-saving construction within a balance of communal, functional and operational priorities.

The University of Nottingham is proud of its architectural heritage. When it acquired a 6-hectare industrial site it decided to develop a campus suitable for its centennial jubilee. Hopkins's competition-winning design created a lake along the site. The principal buildings – three faculties, a learning resource centre and a central teaching building – overlook the lake along a path that leads to the university's playing fields and original campus.

There is also accommodation for 850 student rooms, organised in five halls.

Colonnades on the pathside buildings engage pedestrians and invite them to look into the gardens and atria located between the finger-like wings. Ground floors accommodate functions such as catering, shops and meeting places; above are faculty rooms. The unusual shapes of the freestanding, circular, learning resource centre and conical lecture halls, which appear to float in the atrium of the central teaching building, proclaim their importance. Halls of residence have more privacy, those for undergraduates adopting a traditional courtyard layout while the one for postgraduates is crescent-shaped.

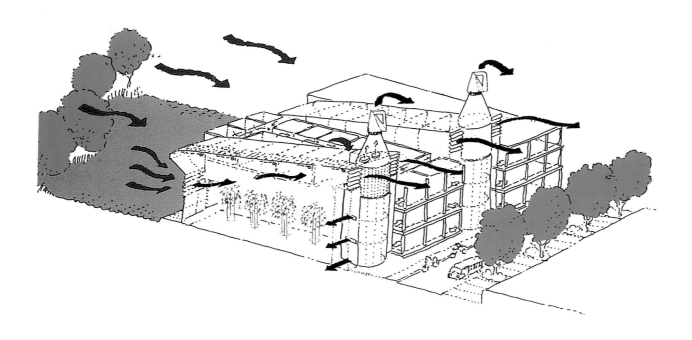

Air flow diagram

General view

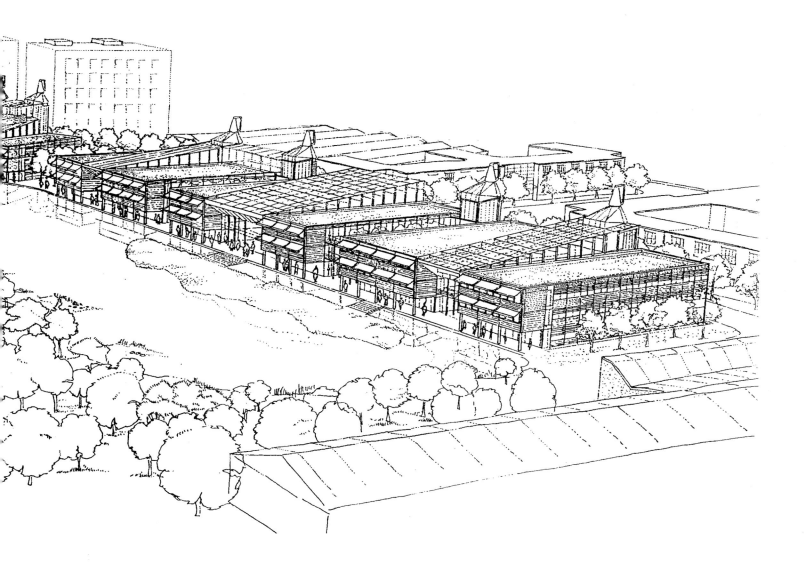

A low-pressure drop-ventilation system uses corridors and stair towers as air plenums, reducing the energy needed to circulate air. Under normal conditions specially designed chimneys create adequate wind effect; during hot weather photovoltaic cells on the roofs of the atria generate supplementary power for extra cooling. Such ideas attracted the largest ever Thermi Grant from the European Union, which allowed a small premium above the stringent cost guidelines for academic buildings, and ensured that the new campus is a worthy companion to the original one.

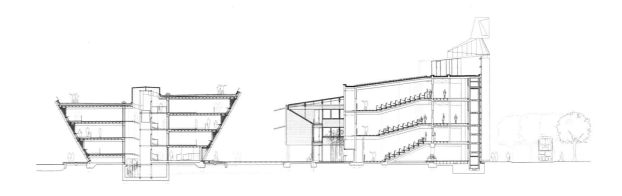

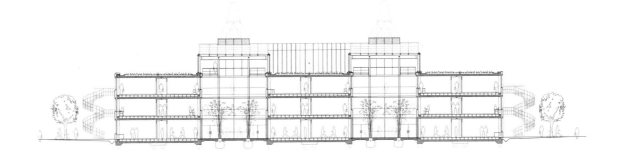

Sections

MICHAEL HOPKINS AND PARTNERS
UNIVERSITY OF CAMBRIDGE
EMMANUEL COLLEGE, QUEEN'S BUILDING

Cambridge, United Kingdom

Emmanuel College, Cambridge, is an enchanted warren of courts. A discreet arch marks the entrance to each, making their thresholds a unique discovery. When glimpsed through a rebuilt colonnade, straddling a passage into the Fellows' Garden, the Queen's Building is the height of this enchantment; it achieves the almost impossible by making the distinction between old and new seem irrelevant. Deceptively simple in form, both freestanding with a continuous arcade around it and yet responsive to its neighbouring structures, its volume is comparable to Wren's chapel while its long axis responds to Leonard Stoke's North Court across Emmanuel Street. It is a seemingly effortless synthesis of old and new, both inviting yet reticent, expressive yet enigmatic.

Previously one of the unloved spaces within the college, the site of the Queen's Building fronts Emmanuel Street and is situated between the Fellows' Garden and the Old Library, adjoining the Master's Lodge. The new building, similar in size and scale to the Wren chapel, breaks with the traditional orthogonal geometry of Front Court and New Court. It is set up on axis, and parallel, to Leonard Stoke's North Court building across Emmanuel Street. This device is intended to help link and draw North Court into the body of the college and provide an important new connection in the sequence of spaces between the Fellows' Garden and the Front Court.

The building accommodates a new 150-seat lecture and performance space for the college, with a raked auditorium and surrounding gallery. The acoustic design is primarily for chamber music and small orchestral groups, but is adjustable for lectures and cinema and theatre performances. The upper levels include a reception room for use with the auditorium and a new middle common room. A quiet reading room and a number of small seminar and music practice rooms are entered from an open colonnade which rings the building at ground level.

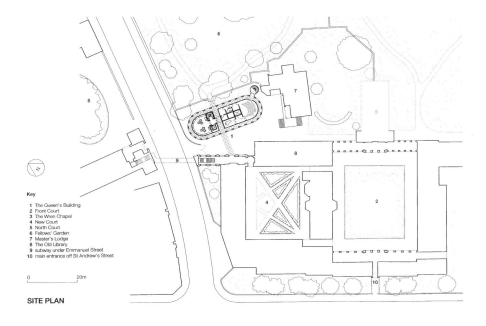

Key

1 The Queen's Building
2 Front Court
3 The Wren Chapel
4 New Court
5 North Court
6 Fellows' Garden
7 Master's Lodge
8 The Old Library
9 subway under Emmanuel Street
10 main entrance off St Andrew's Street

0   20m

SITE PLAN

Site plan

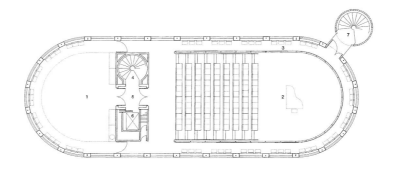

0   5m

SECOND FLOOR

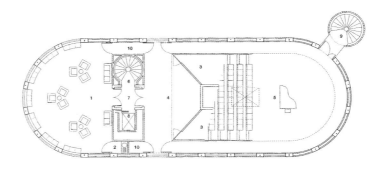

0   5m

FIRST FLOOR

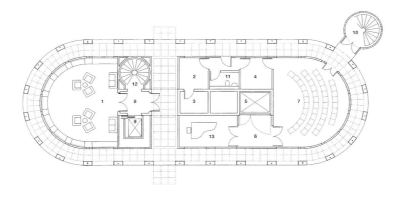

0   5m

GROUND FLOOR

Like the Wren chapel, the new building is made from Ketton limestone, but the frame is formed with openings large enough for the structure to be recognised as having been constructed at the end of the 20th-century using a technique that combines the compressive strength of the stone for the external walls with the spanning potential and mass of concrete for the floors. The concrete is expressed at the bearing nodes in the walls. The roof, which employs steel and timber trusses to support a heavy timber acoustic roof, is finished in lead.

The Queen's Building transcends the old dualities of modern versus traditional, and old versus new, in a pristine composition which is full of delightful surprises and intellectual satisfaction.

The design balances tradition and innovation. The Ketton limestone walls form a smooth plane in which each mark and opening deliberately speaks of construction; the columns diminish as they carry less load; the infill panels are clearly incised and made from larger, flatter stones; the single large window on the first floor reveals the location of the entrance. All is held together by steel rods, whose junctions are deliberately expressed in the tie rings cast into the concrete pad stones – a device that suggests an equilibrium between dynamic forces. The interior elaborates on this sense of balance; it comprises two common rooms, a greenroom and ancillary spaces on the lower floors while on top are situated a reception room and a 170-seat auditorium. The volume and raking form of the latter are unexpected and contribute to a potent balance of stone walls, timber seats and roof arranged in a horseshoe form, all of which add intensity to performances; here the sumptuous materials and their exploited potential imbues the whole with a satisfaction which is both sensual and intellectual.

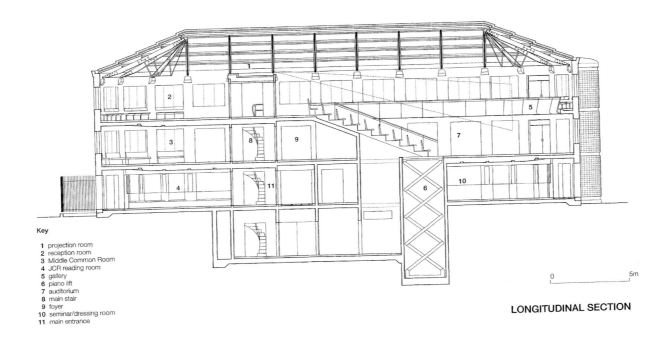

Key

1 projection room
2 reception room
3 Middle Common Room
4 JCR reading room
5 gallery
6 piano lift
7 auditorium
8 main stair
9 foyer
10 seminar/dressing room
11 main entrance

0   5m

LONGITUDINAL SECTION

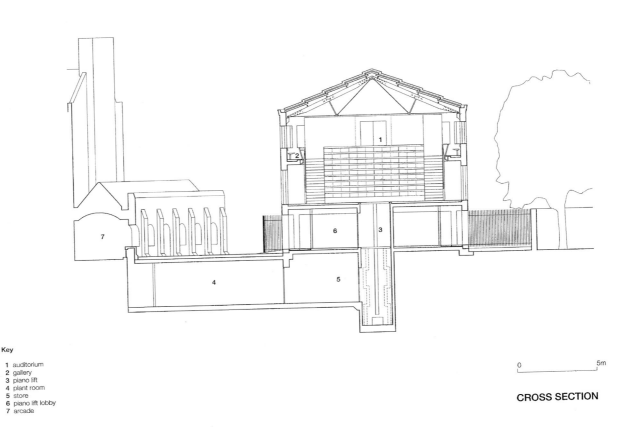

Key

1 auditorium
2 gallery
3 piano lift
4 plant room
5 store
6 piano lift lobby
7 arcade

0   5m

CROSS SECTION

MECANOO

UTRECHT POLYTECHNIC FACULTY OF ECONOMICS AND MANAGEMENT

Utrecht, The Netherlands

The building is situated in the so-called kasbah zone of the Utrecht campus. The kasbah, a traditional feature of North African cities, is characterised by compact, low-level buildings and beautifully tended courtyards. Following this model, the three-storey building is designed to enclose three new courtyards.

To create a building that is more than just an educational facility it is important to give students an opportunity to gather informally, eat, drink, study or relax. Consequently an informal atmosphere and flexibility are central to this scheme – qualities reflected in the provision of generous circulation spaces that also incorporate areas for meeting. Financial constraints, considered an incentive rather than a problem, gave rise to a design full of surprising contrasts that establish a variety of atmospheres in the building. Oppositions between rough and refined, concrete and wood, complex and simple, can be felt throughout.

The building has a clear organisational structure. On the north side, where the main entrance is located, is the congress zone containing four large lecture rooms, a multimedia library and a restaurant overlooking a canal. The lecture rooms are closed boxes which seem to float within an elongated transparent volume parallel to the street. The boxes are clad with different materials – wood, expanded metal mesh, stucco and metal – so that each has its own character. Between the lecture halls, a series of balconies on different levels can be used for casual conversations, meetings and as waiting areas between lectures.

At right angles to the conference wing are two corridors which give access to classrooms overlooking the central courtyard. Staff and administration offices are situated along the three outer edges and enclose the building on the south, east and west sides. Squares

have been created at the six intersections of the corridors to house each discipline.

The courtyards form the heart of the building help to determine the atmosphere of the surrounding spaces. Each makes its own contribution. In the introverted Zen courtyard, inspired by Japanese gardens for meditation, two kinds of gravel are separated by a steel strip. Fourteen large boulders are carefully placed on the gravel. This composition in stone gives the courtyard a static character which is slightly softened by the presence of two delicate trees. In contrast, the appearance of the water court is one of constant flux. Because of the reflective water surface and the landscape visible through the glass wall at the south end of the courtyard, the atmosphere changes with each season and with the weather. The central jungle courtyard is the liveliest and largest of the three outdoor spaces and the only one which can be entered. At the level of the first floor it is crossed by open steel footbridges with built-in seats. Bamboos of different colours and heights and offering a great variety of leaf texture are allowed to overrun the steel bridges, creating a dynamic ambience.

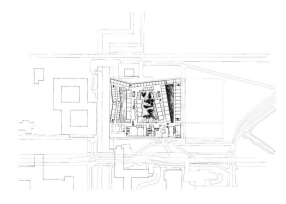

Site plan

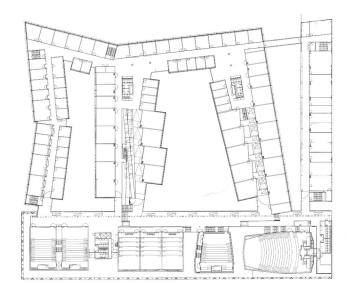

Second floor plan

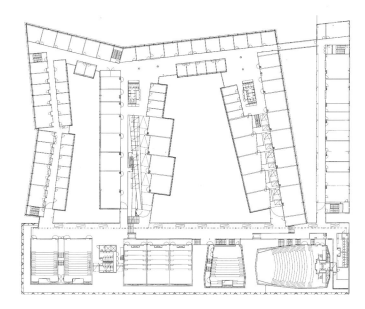

First floor plan

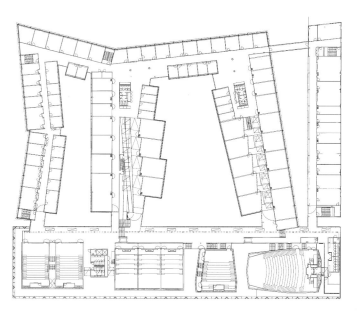

Ground floor plan

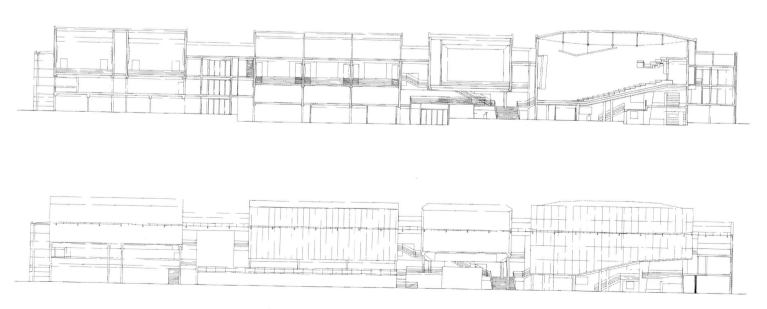

Sections

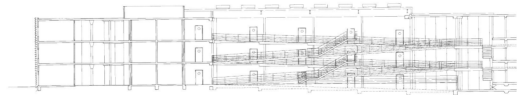

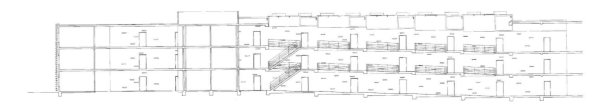

Sections

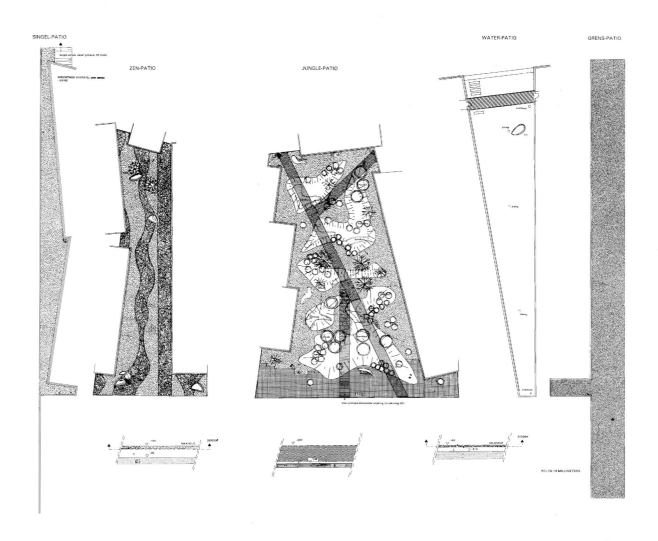

Garden plan

UNIVERSITY OF UTRECHT MINNAERT BUILDING

Utrecht, The Netherlands

Construction of the Minnaert Building is one more step in the process of filling in and linking up the existing network of the northwestern cluster on the de Uithof university campus. The programme for the building comprises three main elements: classrooms and laboratories; a restaurant serving the entire northwestern corner; and workspace for three departments.

This functional programme is complemented by the 'tare space', an undefined area made up of circulation and service zones. The basic idea was to concentrate as much of this as possible in one large attractive hall, transit area and meeting place in the northwestern corner. The area is on the first floor, the *piano nobile*, an expansion tank within the existing circulation network of aerial walkways. Each of the different elements in the programme is allocated a well-defined place around this central hall.

The main feature of the hall is a large 10 metre by 50 metre pond that collects rainwater and is used as the cooling machine for the building. In daytime the water is pumped through the building, absorbing the excessive heat; in the evening it is pumped back to the roof for cooling. During rainy periods, the water cascades noisily into the hall and raises the water level on the sloping floor in a tidal effect. In general, the building is designed around the senses: sound, smell, humidity, wind, darkness and light, heat and cold are used as architectural instruments.

The construction consists of ochre-coloured pre-fabricated concrete elements which allow for large open spaces to be spanned. The facade is covered by an undulating skin of concrete that has been roughly sprayed with a sienna pigment, a treatment that enhances the monolithic character of the building.

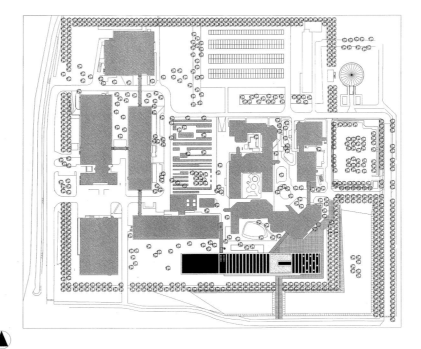

Site plan

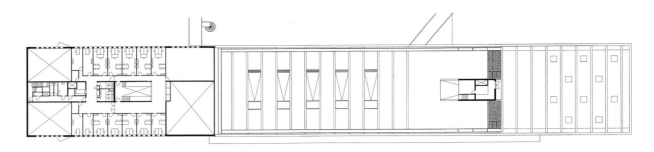

Third floor plan

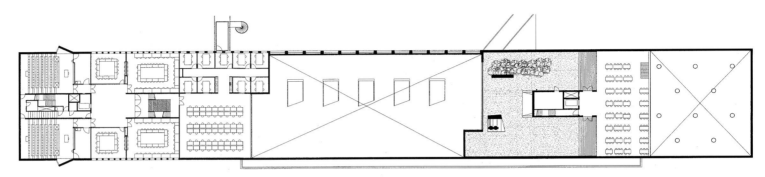

Second floor plan

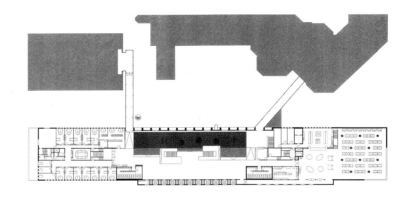

First floor plan

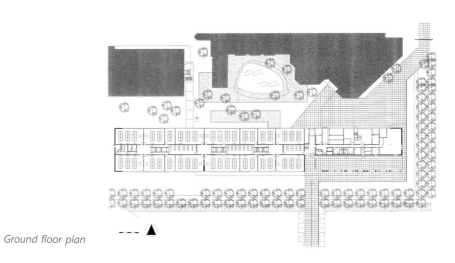

Ground floor plan

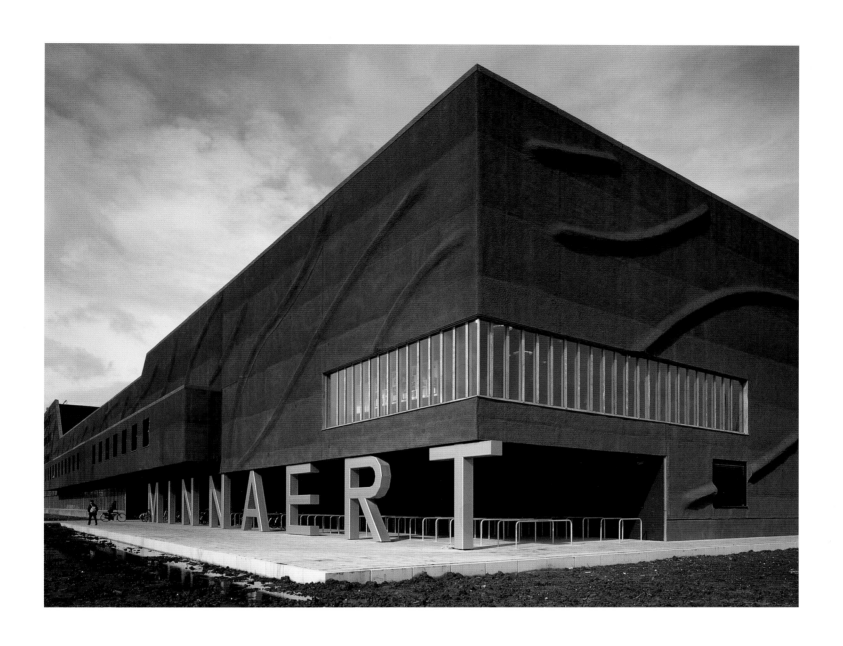

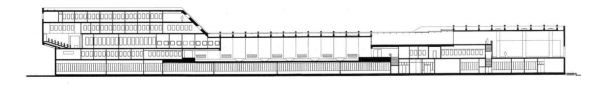

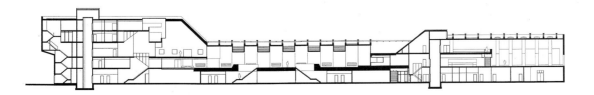

Sections

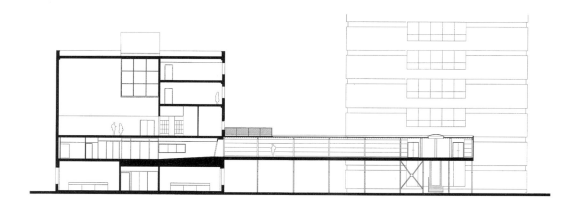

Section

WILLIAM MARSH RICE UNIVERSITY DUNCAN HALL

Houston, Texas, USA

Duncan Hall houses the computational engineering faculty of the School of Engineering, together with Owlnet, the main computer centre for the whole university, and the offices of the dean of engineering. Where the main public rooms are situated around the main hall, the Martell Hall, it serves, in addition, the outreach teaching aspects of the university. The rooms can be used at night without compromising the security of the remainder of the study and seminar rooms of Duncan Hall, which remain accessible to the faculty.

The architectural qualities of Martell Hall and its proximity to Lovett Hall, the site of the 1984 G7 Conference and the original building of the university, have ensured that it is frequently used for major get-togethers, from formal dinners for the founders' committee to informal 'conceptual bazaars' linked to lectures and seminars in the rooms around Martell Hall. The key to this extensive and varied functionality is the utility of the architecture together with the richness of the decoration.

For most of the 20th-century institutionally, conventionality and ritual have been seen as qualities that must either be controlled, reduced/or, if necessary, eliminated. This was because the 'old', 19th-century rituals were seen as dysfunctional. However, experience has shown that public life does not work at all without a high degree of formality, even if it is dressed up as informality!

In Duncan Hall, the architects have devised a new 'order', which they christened a 'working order', that combines the three Vitrubian functions with the single (trabeated) element of column and beam. The effect of this is to revise radically the idea of Functionalism as the predominant style of modernity. Instead of functionality flowing from designing space so as to make it 'work better' it simply flows from a radically redesigned 'architectural order'. The room spaces are 'served' directly by the order and their level of

functionality is defined mainly by what the order provides. This is because the working order is a circulation corridor, an electromechanical service duct and both frame and field to 'iconic engineering'. These three functions: of engineering the social, the physical, and the conceptual environment correspond to the Vitruvian functions of commodity, firmness and delight.

This design strategy liberates room spaces from the restrictive straitjacket of specific and peculiar form sought by the architectural philosophy of Functionalism. This liberation of the room space is a licence for it to be either dull and neutral or wild and surprising. Whatever form rooms take, the 'service order' ensures that they will be provided with as much functionality as the budget can afford. The accessibility of the order, in its role as a duct, also allows services to be added and changed, so increasing the functions available in any room.

The architecture at Rice University is proof that the taboos of conventional 20th-century Modernism can be broken, exploded and discarded. The supposedly useless device of an architectural order can be redesigned to be, instead of a mere ornament, the essential provider of all the utilities. The supposedly impossible task of decoration – to promulgate ideas that are shared by all who live today – can be solved aesthetically by using the supermarket graphics descended from normative 20th-century art whether abstract or Cubist in concept. The problem of their content can also be solved by employing current ideas in science and metaphysics. One would have no problem with redesigning the conceptual environment, should that radically change, in just the way one installs a new service provider. This is why, while some people might refer to the building's ceiling, designed by Steve and Sue Shaper, as 'art', the architects prefer to call it 'iconic engineering'.

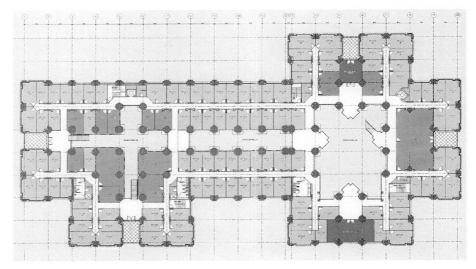

Second floor plan

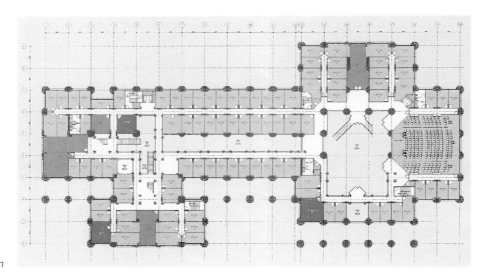

First floor plan

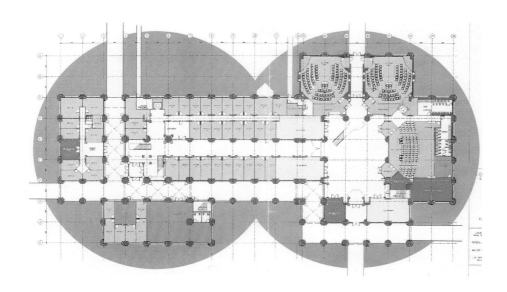

Ground floor plan

Section

JOHN OUTRAM

UNIVERSITY OF CAMBRIDGE, JUDGE INSTITUTE OF MANAGEMENT STUDIES

Cambridge, United Kingdom

Oxbridge is unique in its elevation of the social, and therefore architectural, status of the college above the faculty. College buildings are mainly privately funded; faculty buildings, especially those erected since the Second World War, have been state funded. The Judge Institute breaks with these traditions, being the first large privately funded faculty. It is architecturally ambitious. It also seeks to promote a new kind of loyalty to the faculty equivalent to that inspired by the college courtyard.

The institute is built on to the 19th-century City Hospital, which is preserved under statute, and is likely to be the last large-scale development allowed in the medieval centre of Cambridge. This suits our architectural project, which is to invent a modern architecture that 'futureproofs' the architectural tradition on its own terms. We show that our invention of a new architectural order, the Working Order ©, can be

seamlessly grafted on to a 19th-century Romanesque building. We prove that this order can, while being functionally an urban megastructure, do so while generating three new buildings, called the Gallery, Castle and Ark respectively, each of which has a completely different scale, height, function and detailed decoration.

The Gallery constitutes the faculty social space. We call this a 'republic of the valley'. It is walled, like an opera house, with seminar balconies which are six-person 'cafe society' openworking spaces, designed to encourage informal dialogue with passers-by.

Up to 200 people can openwork on the six floorplates of the 36 metre long by 26 metre high solar spiral Gallery. The roof is solid, which avoids air refrigeration in summer. The sun enters the high space by sidelight in the morning. The space is shaded at midday by exterior 'light shelves', and in the afternoon,

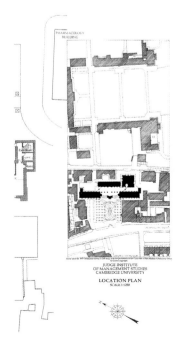

Location plan

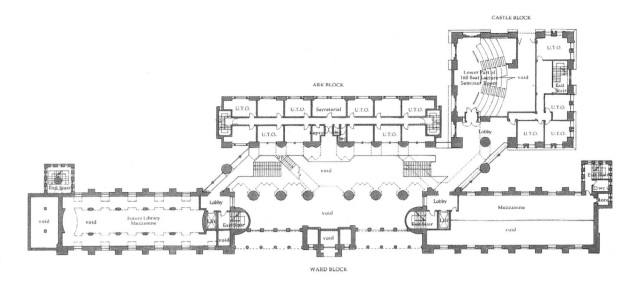

*Second floor
plan*

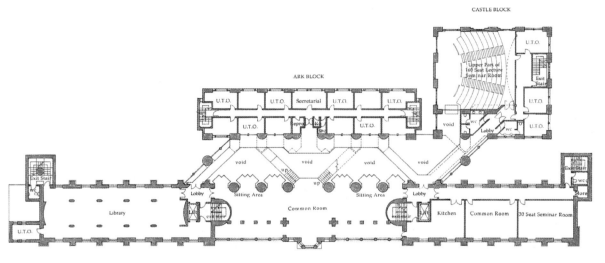

First floor plan

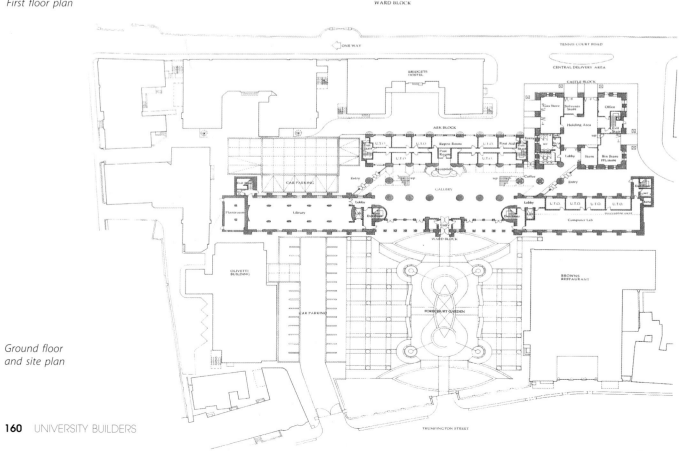

*Ground floor
and site plan*

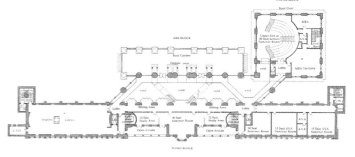

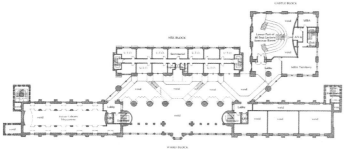

Third floor plan

Fourth floor plan

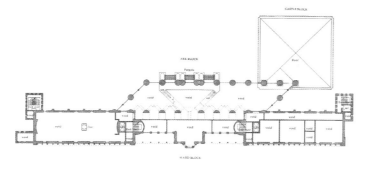

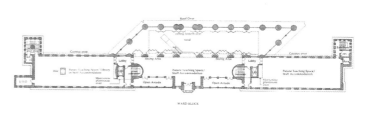

Fifth floor plan

Sixth floor plan

Section

OLIVETTI   JUDGE INSTITUTE OF MANAGEMENT STUDIES   BRIDGET'S HOSTEL   TENNIS COURT ROAD   DOWNING COLLEGE

ERIC PARRY ARCHITECTS
SUSSEX INNOVATION CENTRE
Falmer, Brighton, United Kingdom

The Sussex Innovation Centre serves as an incubator for the development and application of good ideas. The building is well positioned at the boundary of the university campus and so reinforces the intention to provide a catalyst to bridge the divide between theory and practice, academia and business.

The finished building developed as a result of three principal influences: the topography of the site; the building form; and the sense of community.

To the west of the site the plan of the centre is defined by, and defines, a new public space created by raising and retaining an area from the natural slope which overlooks the university buildings designed by Sir Basil Spence. To the south, the car park lies below this raised plateau, while to the east the brick wall and roof mark the boundary of the campus.

In plan the building form is a deceptively simple two-storey rectangle 60 metres long and 17.5 metres wide and split into 10 equal bays. The building is naturally ventilated and passively controlled and therefore the width is critical for cross-ventilation. The developed solution increases the normal dimension by the triple use of the central spine for circulation, lighting and ventilation.

To create a communal atmosphere there is a deliberate openness to the common parts – the café, the entrance, the conference rooms – and to the way in which interior passages open onto the rest of the building.

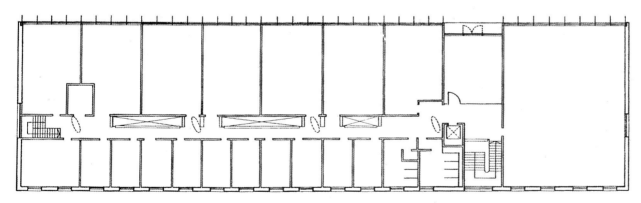

Floor plan

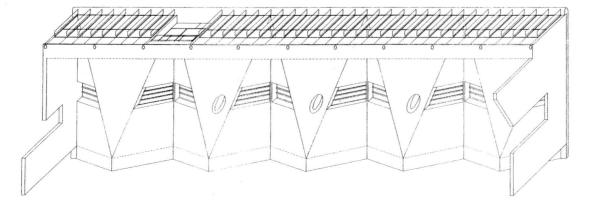

Isometric axonometric of roof

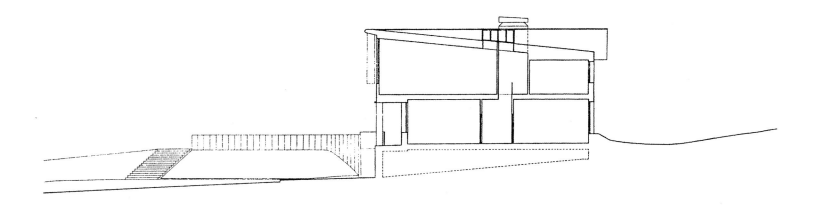

Section

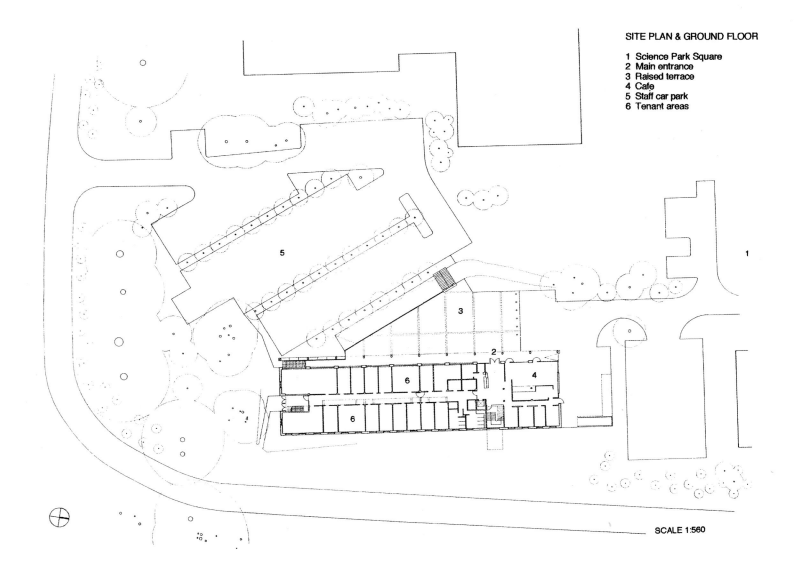

SITE PLAN & GROUND FLOOR

1 Science Park Square
2 Main entrance
3 Raised terrace
4 Cafe
5 Staff car park
6 Tenant areas

SCALE 1:560

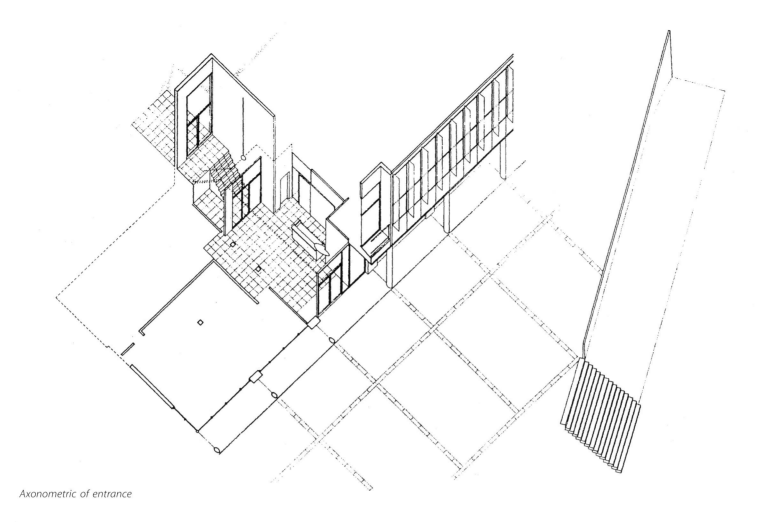

Axonometric of entrance

ANTOINE PREDOCK ARCHITECT

UCSB STUDENT AFFAIRS AND ADMINISTRATIVE SERVICES BUILDING

Santa Barbara, California, USA

As a gateway to the University of California at Santa Barbara, the student affairs and administrative services building acknowledges the architectural and urbanistic qualities fostered in the original campus, while creating a new, dynamic crossroads designed to promote the interaction of arriving students, the existing student body and the UCSB administrative services. The reinterpretation of the local Santa Barbara block building material into a running bond format allows the building to express itself as a facility which houses administrative functions while celebrating the variety of those functions as they serve the student body.

The building is sited at the terminus of the primary pedestrian thoroughfare and straddles the main entry into the campus. It accommodates a variety of student-related services. Essentially an open courtyard building, the plan organises itself along two desire lines: the student axis into the campus and the cross-axis of connection to the existing administration block. Given the symbolic individuality of the axis and the require-ment of each department to have its own front door, the building prioritises itself in plan and section through analysis of existing and projected visitor and user volume. The resultant design expresses the dynamic of this volumetric analysis as it manifests itself in plan, section and elevation.

Programmatic requirements for departmental indi-viduality and the mild, forgiving climate of the Santa Barbara area enable the building to be served by exterior circulation. With this strategy, the courtyard becomes the building lobby, promoting a multifunc-tional space for students, faculty and administrative activities. While the courtyard possesses the attributes of the lobby, the visitor centre acts as the front door of the building and the symbolic gateway to the campus for incoming students and faculty. The interaction of the visitor centre and the student and administrative services departments with the courtyard space will provide for, and foster, an environment of under-standing, respect and excitement for the educational process.

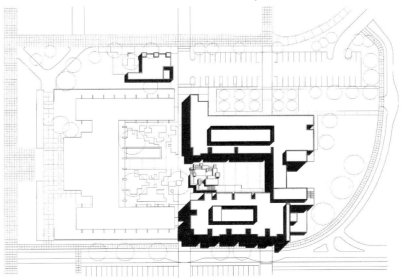

Site plan

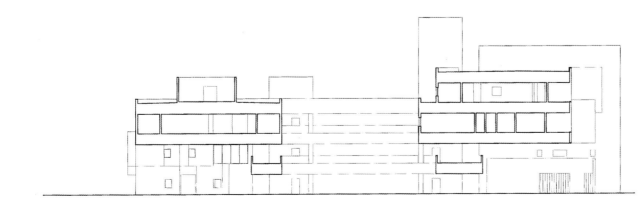

Section

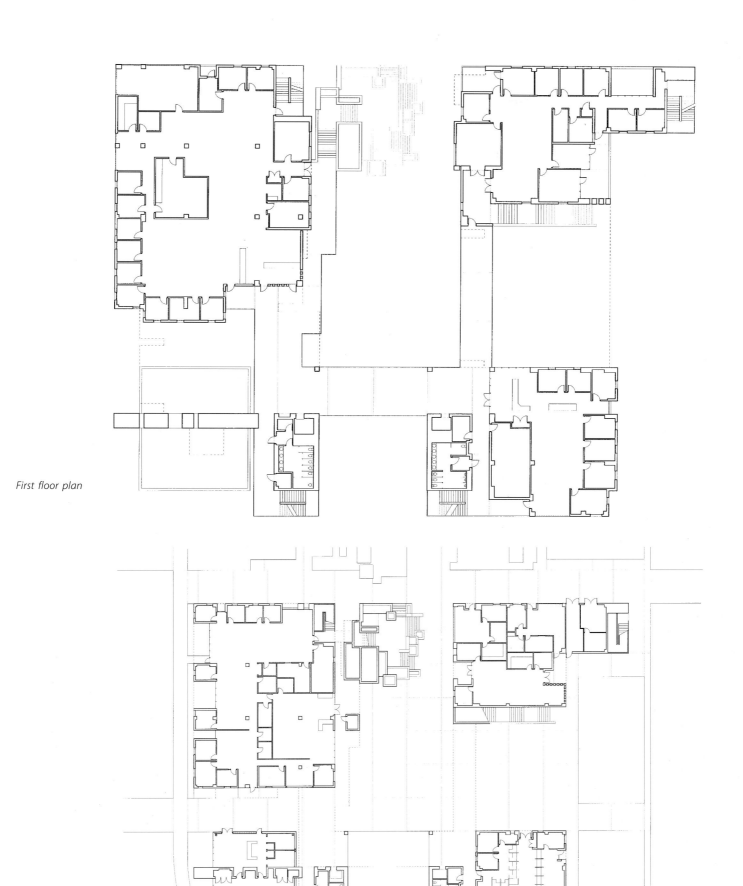

First floor plan

Ground floor plan

ANTOINE PREDOCK ARCHITECT
UCSC FACULTY OF MUSIC
Santa Cruz, California, USA

The campus of University of California, Santa Cruz is blessed with a magnificent natural setting. Overlooking the city of Santa Cruz and Monterey Bay, it has evolved, through a fascinating series of geological events, into richly varied ecosystems of forest, ravine and meadow, each possessing its own landforms, vegetation and wildlife; the textural transition is from mossy redwood forest to alternately sun-drenched or foggy meadow tempered by stately oak.

The 4-acre music faculty site is bounded to the east by meadow and to the west by the performing arts complex. Sited to respect the low, grassy hills, the building digs into, and rests low on the meadow. To the north and east, bermed walls visually bring the meadow over the building. The large masses of the recital and concert halls are to the southwest where the terrain begins to fall away. As the mass of the building generally retains a low profile, it respects view corridors of the building to the north while commanding a sweeping view of Monterey Bay. To fully benefit from this vantage point the building splits, creating an outdoor area with a view to the meadow and the bay beyond. Where natural views are not possible, internal courtyards allow light to penetrate faculty offices and practice rooms.

A solitary oak tree, a promontory on the grassland meadow, focuses the entry court. From here, students, faculty and audience members take separate entrances to the 400-seat recital hall, the gamelan pavilion or the academic facility. The 1,500-seat concert hall, to be constructed as a later phase, has a separate ceremonial approach. Special attention has been given to the highly technical acoustic requirements of the various performance, teaching, office and practice spaces for the university's music department. The music village is a series of spaces enhanced by courtyards, ravines and exterior decks. These outdoor areas lend themselves to becoming impromptu meeting places, exterior practice areas and alternative performance sites.

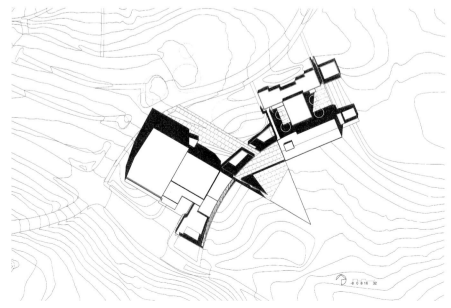

Site plan

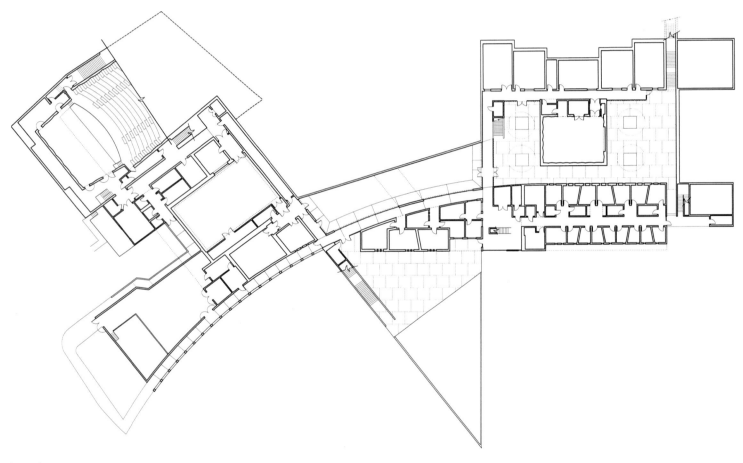

Floor plan

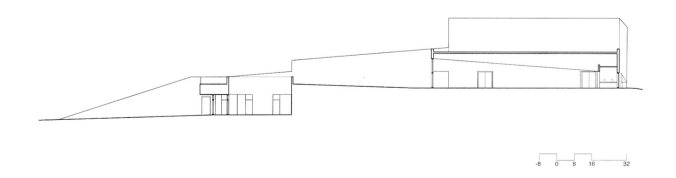

Section

-8 0 8 16 32

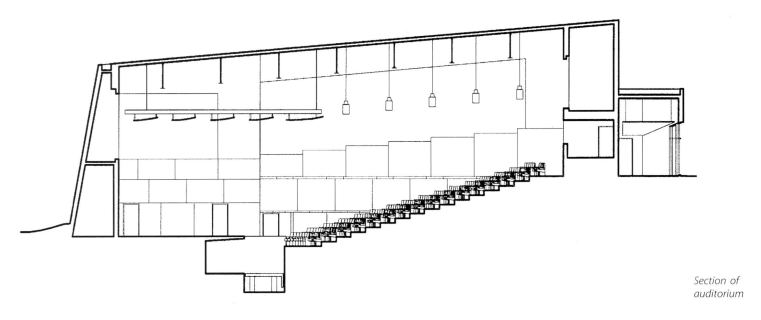

Section of auditorium

THAMES VALLEY UNIVERSITY, LEARNING RESOURCE CENTRE

Slough, United Kingdom

Landlocked and separated from the centre by a major roundabout junction and the tracks of the London Paddington to Bristol line, the campus comprises a selection of purpose-designed high- and low-rise buildings constructed between the mid-1950s and early 1970s. The thrust of the masterplan is to reinforce the orthogonal layout of the existing buildings and the spaces between with landscaping and to identify sites for new buildings, to create a campus that supports a cohesive relationship between buildings and landscape, creating clear circulation routes.

From the masterplan study, a site for the new learning resource centre was identified on an area which at the time was occupied by an engineering workshop built in the mid-1950s. A brief was evolved, in conjunction with Thames Valley University, for a 3,500m^2 building, housing books, videos and CD-ROMs which would also include space for laptop computers, open working areas and enclosed seminar rooms. Apart from meeting budgetary constraints and

adhering to a fast construction programme, the building was to epitomise the university's ethos that learning and knowledge should be both accessible and enjoyable. The brief generated a simple diagram for the building with service and storage areas, in a warehouse block referred to as the 'bookstack', contrasted with an open reading and entrance area within a lofty space covered by a curved roof. The ground floor is raised by 1.5 metres to provide an uninterrupted procession between new and existing buildings.

The building consists of three elements: the bookstack below, the curved roof and the surrounding landscape. The detail design and construction of each element had to be kept simple to meet budgetary demands while, to maintain the architectural clarity of each element, the structure had to be energy efficient within a computer-oriented environment.

The bookstack is an *in situ* fair-faced concrete frame stripped of any covering metal spandrel panels. The external cladding is set within the concrete frame and

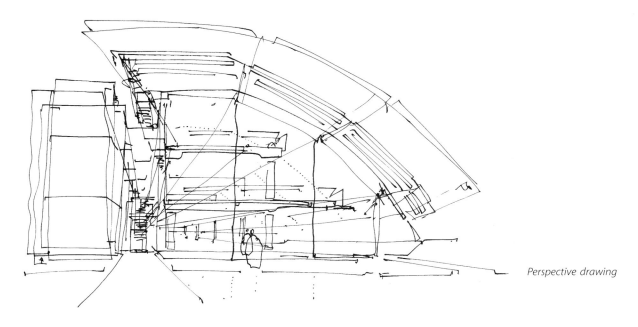

Perspective drawing

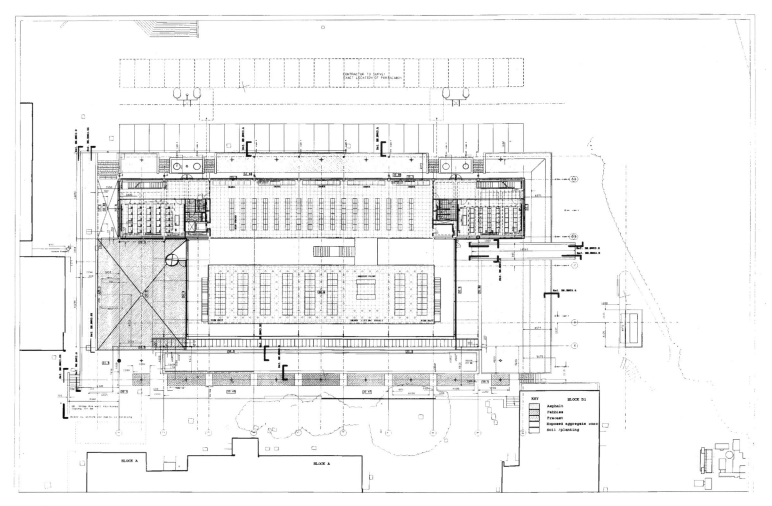

Floor plan

consists of fixed and openable double-glazed panels on the southwest and north with solid insulated panels on the east side, except for the ground-floor café which is set behind an open galvanised grille whose transparency modulates to provide varying amounts of light and shade. On the west facade, maximum shading is provided for the reading areas, which are naturally ventilated by manually opening windows. To allow more light to enter the seminar rooms, the grilles' cells are more open. Cantilevered brackets attached to the cladding support the extruded aluminium channel, which expresses the raised floor while providing a fixed zone for the block gallery-balustrading.

The curved roof construction comprises primary curved beams bearing on to steel brackets fixed to the concrete frame and the ground. Purlins span across these beams, hidden internally by a perforated trapezoidal lining and visible externally as a profiled cantilever that supports a canopy on the south formed by the outer curved Kalzip aluminium sheeting.

A glazed strip running parallel to the bookstack articulates the junction between it and the curved roof. This rooflight provides natural daylight to the central aisle on the ground floor as well as to the perimeter of levels one and two and the deck. Solar control is provided by internal motorised fabric blinds running along tensioned wire guides. The 40 metre-long window running parallel to the external pond has automatically opening top vents for ventilation and is of the same construction as the top rooflight. This window affords wonderful serene views of the pond from the ground and level one deck above: glistening water, darting goldfish and swaying reeds. The volume contained by the curved roof and bookstack offers views of the sky above, the pond and planting to the east and views through the glazed north and south gable walls.

The gable end wall, curved on top, rises to a height of 12 metres with restraint to wind loading provided by fabricated steel mullions, with top connection detail to allow relative movement of the curved roof.

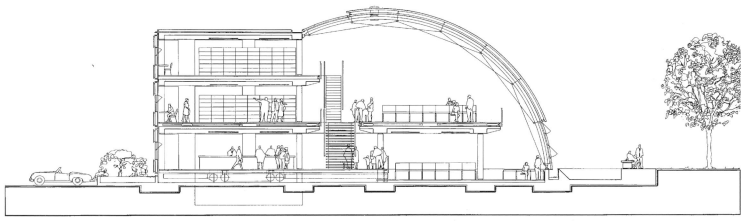

Section

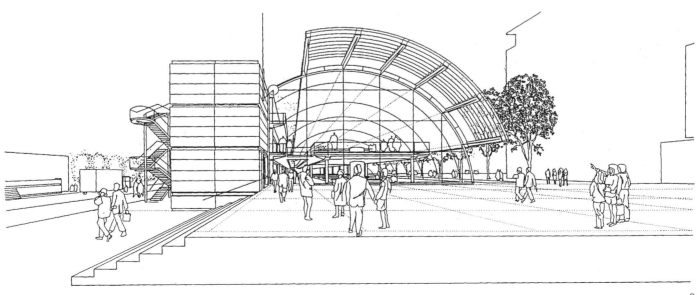

Projection

DE MONTFORT UNIVERSITY QUEEN'S BUILDING

Leicester, United Kingdom

The School of Engineering and Manufacture at De Monfort University is rehoused within the all-new 10,000m² Queen's Building which opened in October 1993. It was designed to be a low-energy structure. Teaching and research at the school related directly to the practical business of manufacturing technology, particularly in the textile industry, hence many of the activities are heat-producing on a prodigious scale. The conventional response would seem to be seal and air-condition a structure of this type. However, this building is almost wholly naturally lit and naturally cross- and stack-ventilated. It was awarded the UK Green Building of the year Award for 1995.

In excess of 2,000 undergraduates, graduates, research students, fellows and staff are connected with the building. Built very precisely to meet the strict Polytechnic & Colleges Funding Council cost and space limits, its construction cost was £8.5 million, excluding fitting out. The university very deliberately describes it as a School of Engineering and Manufacture. Because teaching and research relate to manufacturing technology, the building replicates typical computer, laboratory and factory situations.

In concerts, the client's ideas for academic reintegration, the city authority's urban design notions and the architect's environmental strategy suggested a series of fundamental configurations: a tight courtyard of electronics laboratories is introduced to the north-west of the site, the 'poor' orientation maintaining a sump of cooler air to cross-ventilate the laboratories, while a large single-volume mechanical engineering hall is placed at the opposite end of the school. The two are connected by a 50-metre-long double-height general laboratory in which mechanical and electronics engineers combine forces to invent new applications of robotics, mechatronics and artificial vision to related production fields. A full-height concourse forms the main circulation space in which many of the very important informal meetings and discussions occur. Its air volume stabilises the thermal behaviour of the surrounding spaces.

Two full-raked amphitheatres, each accommodating 160 people, are sited above similar, radial plan, flat-floored teaching rooms. Their ceiling slabs support north-lit drawing and design studios, half of which are devoted to CAD and half to drawing or board design activity. General purpose classrooms occupy the ground floor, supported by a computer node and common room. Staff and research fellows occupy the attics encircling the design studios. A specialist engine test cell sits a little apart from the main building on Mill lane.

Short & Associates believe that a natural conditioning strategy may promote a more flexible and sympathetic approach to urban planning. Their hypothesis is that the optimal form for such a building dissolves its considerable volumes into narrow sectional elements, with free elevation on two or even three sides. We believe that it is possible for such a building, while it is attempting to strike a rhythm with its immediate environment, also to exploit its inherently more flexible form to mend a hole in the surviving urban fabric.

The more manoeuvrable building volumes resulting from the notion of introducing light and air from both sides and above enable, for example, the street elevation to flex so as to reinforce the old city routes while tuning the orientation of the various elements. The drawing studios are very deliberately slewed to create north-lit spaces, and receive high levels of diffuse indirect light.

Crucial to the environmental strategy is the thermal stability provided by the massive brick masonry construction. Furthermore, this masonry must be

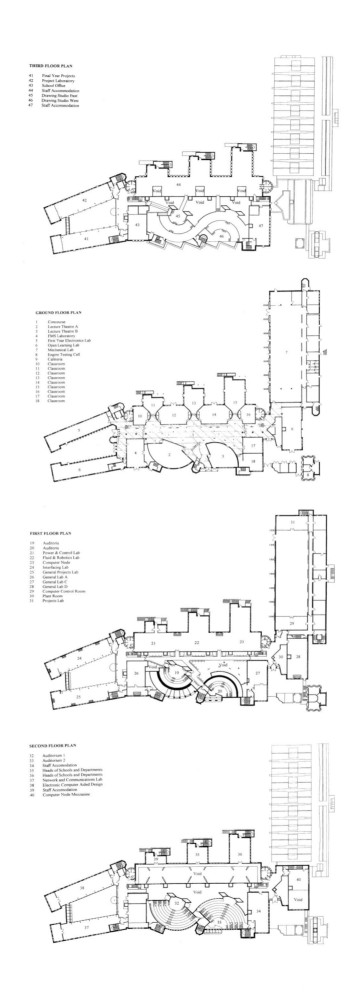

THIRD FLOOR PLAN

41   Final Year Projects
42   Project Laboratory
43   School Office
44   Staff Accommodation
45   Drawing Studio East
46   Drawing Studio West
47   Staff Accommodation

GROUND FLOOR PLAN

1   Concourse
2   Lecture Theatre A
3   Lecture Theatre B
4   FMS Laboratory
5   First Year Electronics Lab
6   Open Learning Lab
7   Mechanical Lab
8   Engine Testing Cell
9   Cafeteria
10   Classroom
11   Classroom
12   Classroom
13   Classroom
14   Classroom
15   Classroom
16   Classroom
17   Classroom
18   Classroom

FIRST FLOOR PLAN

19   Auditoria
20   Auditoria
21   Power & Control Lab
22   Fluid & Robotics Lab
23   Computer Node
24   Interfacing Lab
25   General Projects Lab
26   General Lab A
27   General Lab C
28   General Lab D
29   Computer Control Room
30   Plant Room
31   Projects Lab

SECOND FLOOR PLAN

32   Auditorium 1
33   Auditorium 2
34   Staff Accomodation
35   Heads of Schools and Departments
36   Heads of Schools and Departments
37   Network and Communications Lab
38   Electronic Computer Aided Design
39   Staff Accomodation
40   Computer Node Mezzanine

exposed to the air volume within; its potential for thermal admittance would be very much reduced by a lightweight applied finish. Mellow-grain pink bricks are used externally with silver, buff and red syncopated stripes. Internally solid loadbearing walls are made in calcium silicate bricks in a variety of pastel colours, set in Flemish bond or collar-jointed to fair-faced block-work walls. The polychromatic expression of various bond types reveals their pattern to the student engineers. The greater the degree of polychromatic density, the less the loadbearing element. The mortar colour is matched to the brickwork to increase the apparent sheerness of the masonry planes. Typically, heavy masonry buildings develop a very occluded ground-floor plan. To avoid this the architects borrowed Violle-Le-Duc's notion of propping up masonry above head height. Pin-jointed steel frames located along the length of the concourse lift the masonry ventilation stacks up to first-floor level. The

stacks are highly visible and have become a popular leitmotif of the campus.

The usual cluttered imagery conveyed by the paraphernalia of air conditioning, its grilles and 'penthouse units' is avoided here. Instead, air inlets and extract-stack terminations are designed specifi-cally to be housed within the natural materials of the building. There are small areas of lightweight timber enclosure, heavily insulated and clad in cedar shingles impregnated with an intumescent material. This was one of its first uses on a public building in Britain.

Every space in the building is different, adapted to its orientation, activity and its particular lighting, acoustic and ventilation requirements. The emphasis is on de-institutionalising a very large university school, on reinforcing the *genius loci* of the existing place – which is more powerful than one might think; and on making new places in the same spirit.

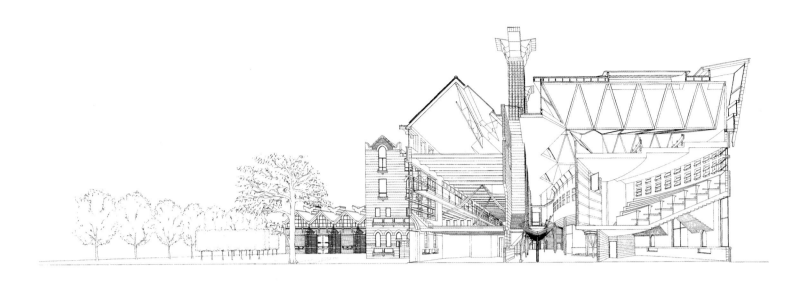

Perspective section

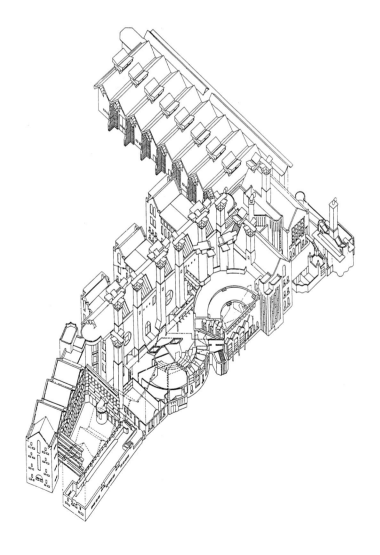

Axonometric

AVEIRO UNIVERSITY DEPARTMENT OF GEOSCIENCES

Aveiro, Portugal

The University of Aveiro is located on a campus site some 70 kilometres south of Oporto, on the Atlantic coast of Portugal. The university boasts a series of new buildings designed by some of the leading Portuguese architects including Alvaro Siza. One of the buildings, the Faculty of Geology, demonstrates clearly the uncompromising rigour that the architect Eduardo Souto de Moura brings to his projects.

The various lecture rooms, laboratories and faculty offices required by the client are ruthlessly marshalled around double-loaded internal corridors on three floors served by two understated stair cores. The ordering system is best understood in section, which is repetitively extruded over the 80 metre length of the building. This horizontal that the client brief required. A plain concrete-finished ceiling and raised access floors allow for the reconfiguration of rooms by the removal and relocation of the dividing walls that run perpen-

dicular to the spine corridor. The longitudinal nature of the building, in section and plan, is dramatically reinforced by the elevation treatment. Supported on a steel framework, ruby-red sections of marble are employed to form a striated *brise soleil*. The resulting extreme horizontal emphasis provides a neutral facade and masks the irregular distribution of rooms behind. This pronounced horizontal effect evokes the surrounding topography of vast flat salt marshes that is the setting for the Aveiro campus, and perhaps makes reference to the building's function, that of studying rock strata.

The Faculty of Geology is a sophisticated and elegant structure, realised by Eduardo Souta de Moura's absolute architectural rigour in the application of a consistent design idea. However, against this uncompromising language one can detect a certain level of architectural wit and clear aesthetic generosity.

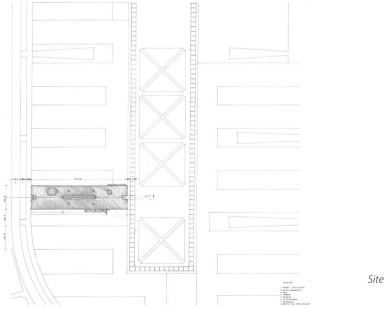

Site plan

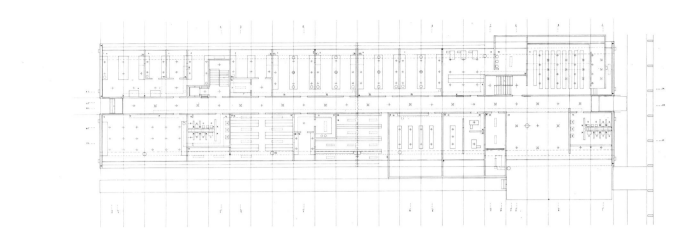

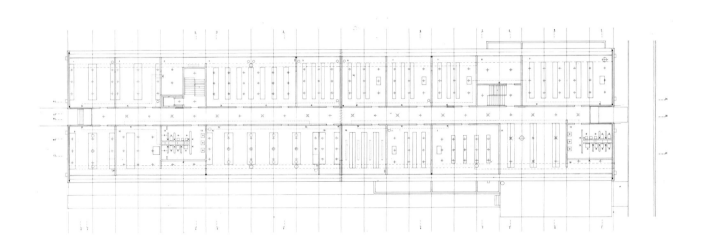

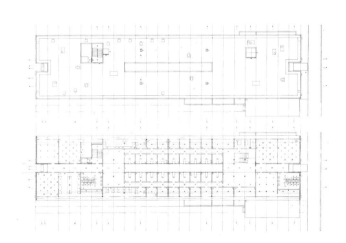

Floor plans

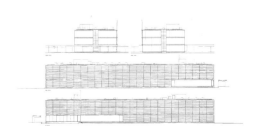

Elevations

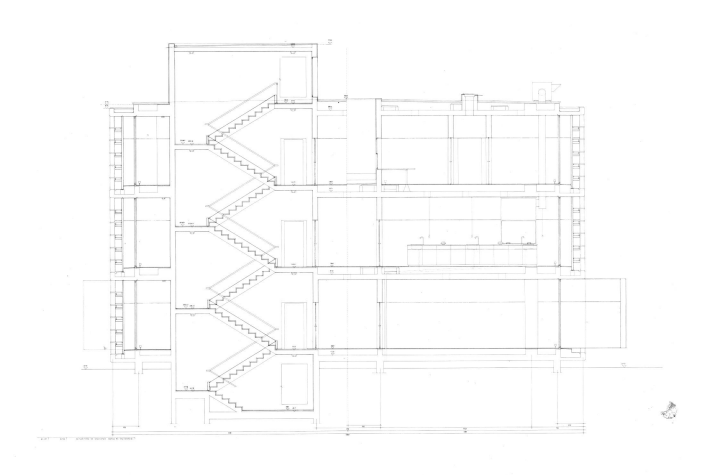

TEMASEK POLYTECHNIC

Singapore

Temasek Polytechnic houses separate schools of applied science, technology, business, and design on a 30-hectare site located between Tampines New Town and Bedok Reservoir at the eastern end of Singapore. The facilities are to accommodate 11,500 students with 1,500 academic and support staff.

The raised entrance plaza, opening towards Tampines Avenue and enclosed by the Horseshoe administration building, is the focus of the campus. It is a public forum, that represents the polytechnic's open relationship with the Singapore community. A large 'window' through the administration building frames a panoramic view towards the reservoir. Public transport is accessed by means of a covered footbridge which connects the plaza to bus shelters situated on either side of Tampines Avenue.

A promenade lined with banks, shops, exhibition galleries and entrances to each of the schools forms the base of the administration building. An auditorium and multipurpose theatre with shared foyer, available for public use and entered from Tampines Avenue, are situated beneath the plaza.

The four schools are organised along pedestrian concourses which radiate from the promenade and are sheltered by upper levels of accommodation that allow for expansion to occur at their extremities. The design optimises vertical and horizontal movement, with densely used spaces such as lecture theatres situated on, or below, concourse level. Each school has its own student canteen overlooking the park.

The plaza, promenade and school concourses form an armature, a pedestrian network that connects academic areas with all facilities less than five minutes'

walk from the centre. Covered ways extend into the landscape alongside the triangular garden and through the park, providing sheltered routes to recreational facilities. A campus road system serves all buildings, car parks and servicing areas with controlled entry from Tampines Avenue at each end of the campus.

Several shared facilities are provided in addition to the academic areas. The highest building is the library tower, which is visible on the Singapore skyline and registers the presence of the polytechnic. The student centre and adjoining central canteen are located on the eastern edge of the triangular garden. The sports hall, stadium and garden containing outdoor pitches and courts are situated at the lower southeastern corner of the campus, while the faculty club, child care centre, swimming pools and staff housing towers enjoy distant views from their site on the higher ground at the western end of the campus.

The contrasting landscapes offered by the plaza parterre, the triangular garden and open parkland ensure variety of experience, a sense of orientation and unify the academic and recreational facilities. Clusters of large trees will shade buildings and parking areas and provide shelter for outdoor study and relaxation.

Local climate and environmental conditions have influenced building orientation, position and scale, hence voids and breezeways create air movement around pedestrian zones.

Temasek campus is a landmark contribution to Singapore's urban architecture with buildings and activities, easily comprehensible to students, staff and visitors, that serve to encourage academic and social interaction.

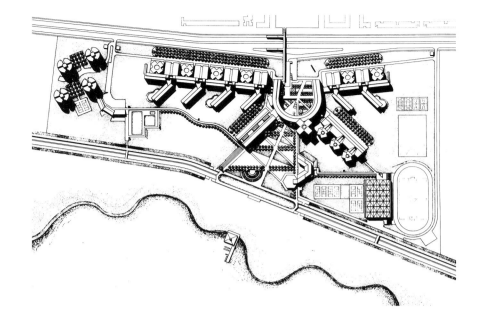

Sire plan

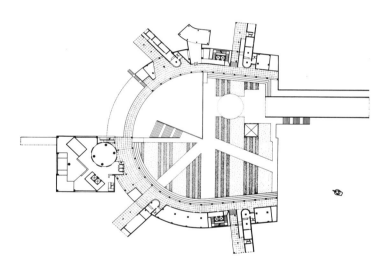

*Horseshoe administration building:
first floor*

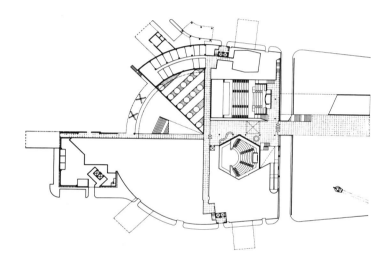

*Horseshoe administration building:
ground floor*

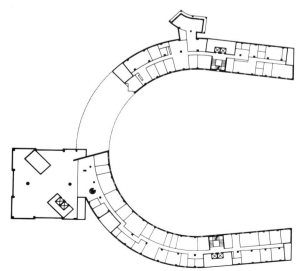

*Horseshoe administration building:
second floor*

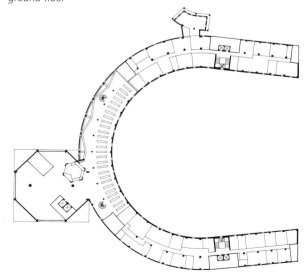

*Horseshoe administration building:
fourth floor plan*

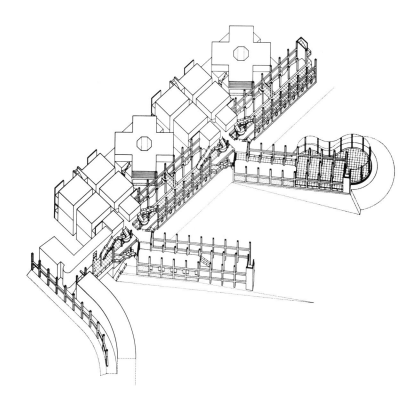

Tampines Avenue building:
axonometric of lower levels

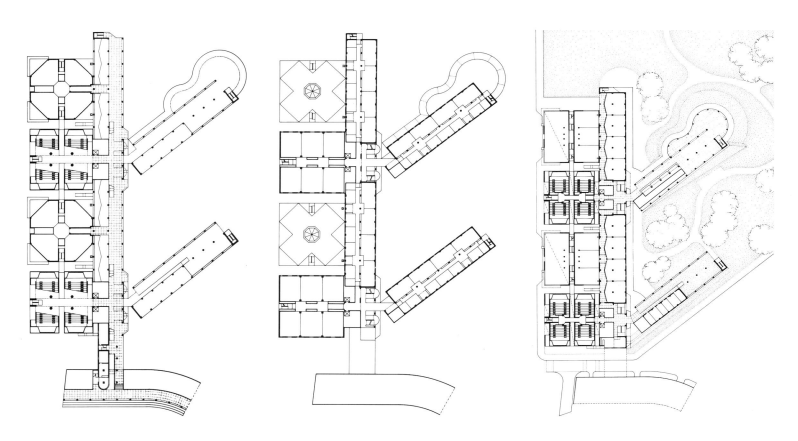

Tampines Avenue building: ground floor, first floor and second floor plans

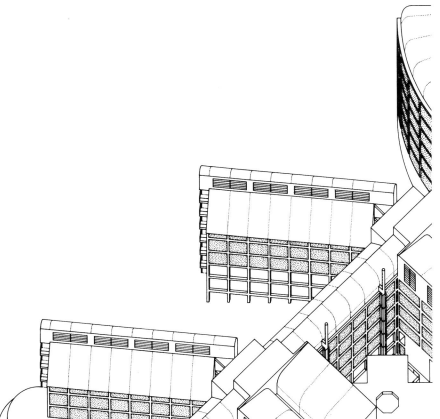

*Tampines Avenue
building:
full axonometric*

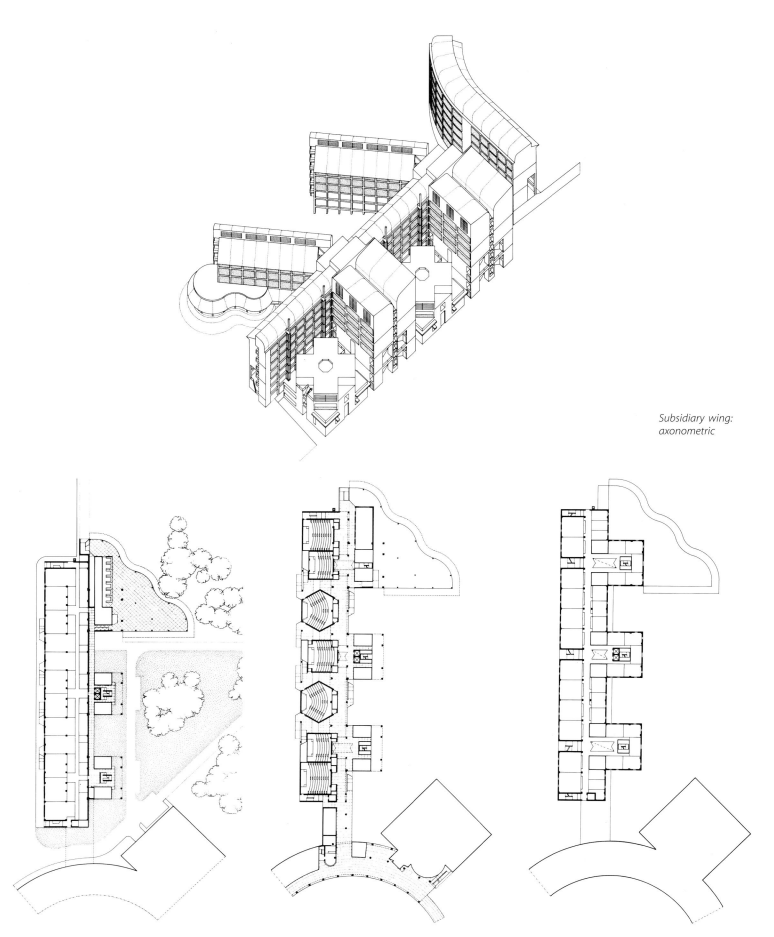

*Subsidiary wing:
axonometric*

Subsidiary wing ground floor, first floor and second floor plans

STUTTGART MUSIC ACADEMY

Stuttgart, Germany

The layout of new buildings and gardens completes the sequence of public institutions and spaces along the 'cultural mile' flanking Konrad-Adenauer-Strasse. The urban composition continues the principle of three-sided external spaces semi-enclosed by buildings opening towards the city, initiated by the original staatsgaleries and mirrored by our new staatsgaleries and theatre garden.

Visitors ascend to the public terrace over the parking garage by ramp and stair from Konrad-Adenauer-Strasse and can enter the theatre academy (the first institution of its kind in Germany) directly or pass into the new plaza to enter the music school and landtag.

Eugenstrasse will become a tree-lined pedestrian route with service vehicle access only. The L-shaped plan of the theatre academy encloses the extended theatre garden on axis with the state theatrem across Konrad-Adenauer-Strasse. The avenue of trees planted along the street will extend the leafy promenade in front of the staatsgaleries.

The urban quality of Urban strasse and Eugenstrasse will be improved as the facades of the new buildings bring the existing unequal heights into unison. The dining room enlivens the corner of Urbanstrasse and Eugenstrasse and is intended as a meeting place for students from both the theatre academy and the music school.

The music school flanks Urbanstrasse and the upper part of Eugenstrasse; it has nine floors with accommodation for students and public. The chamber music/lecture hall, as the concert hall and library are located in the tower – registering the presence of the music school on the city's skyline. The main entrance is from Urbanstrasse into a four-storey foyer which links to the public entrance from the plaza.

The public entrance for concert and chamber music performances is directly into the tower from the plaza. The entrance to the theatre academy is from the Konrad-Adenauer-Strasse terrace close to the theatre arch. The foyer houses a reception area, ticket office and cloakrooms and leads to a fully equipped teaching theatre. Sound studios and workshops are situated on lower levels related to the stages. Dressing rooms with make-up and wig-making departments form the remainder of the backstage accommodation.

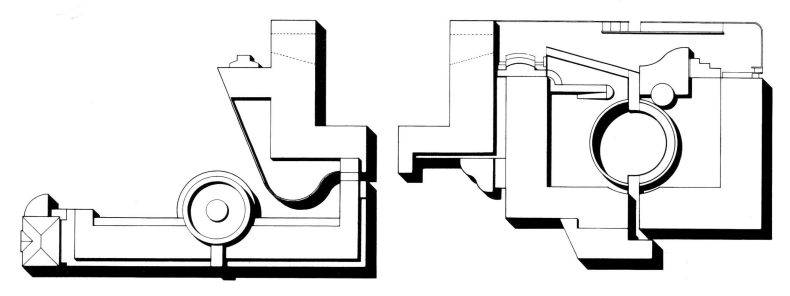

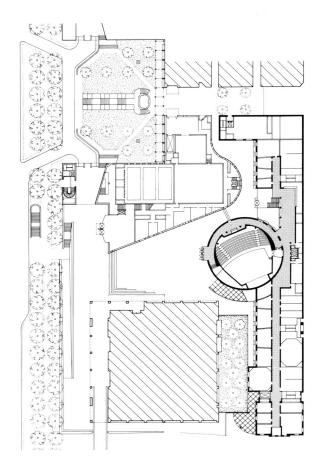

Ground floor plan

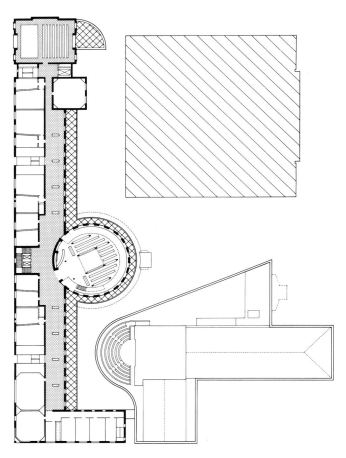

Second floor plan

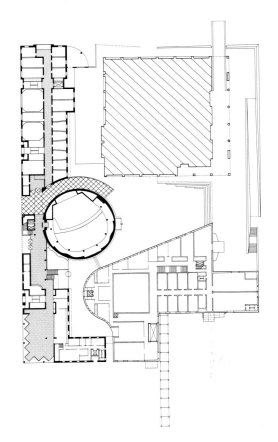

First floor plan

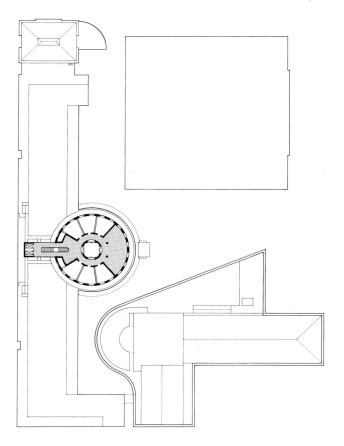

Third floor plan

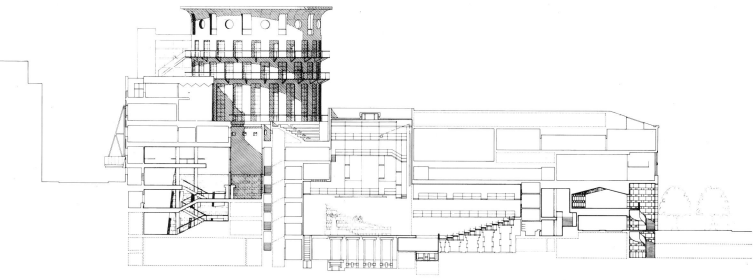

Section

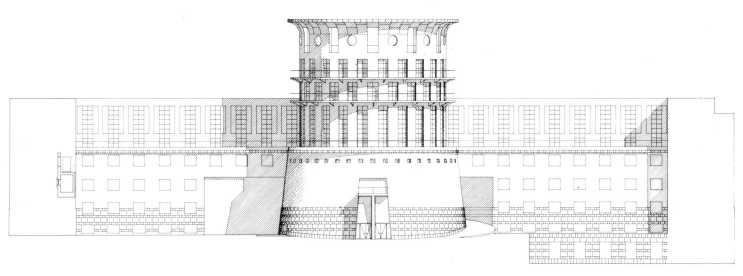

Elevation

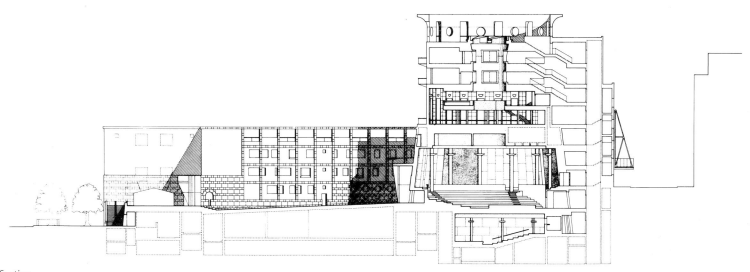

Section

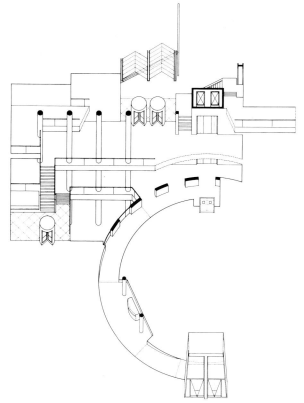

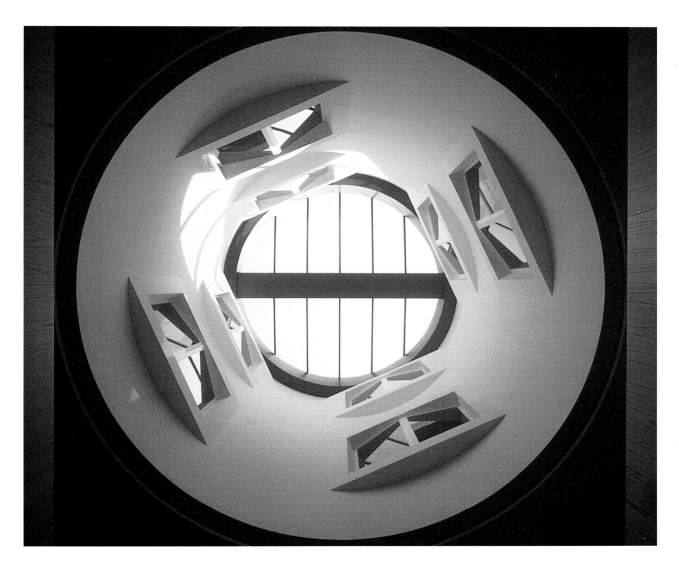

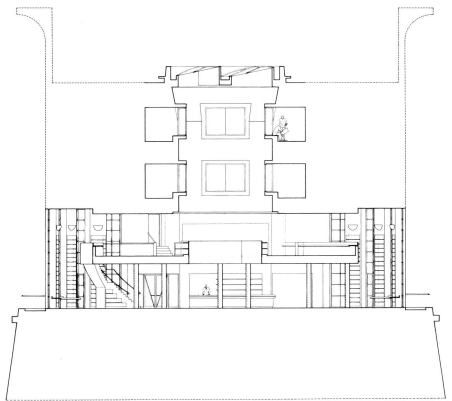

Section

PROJECT INFORMATION

The following information has been correlated from material provided by the architects. All costs and measurements should be taken as a guide only.

Ahrends Burton & Koralek

Dublin Dental Hospital, Trinity College, Dublin, Ireland
Type of commission: competitive interview
Project team: Mary Cornerford, Paul Drake, Michelle Fagan, Aaron Fletcher, Paul de Freine, Mick Haley, Paul Koralek, Socrates Miltiadou, Dave O'Shea, Christine Price, Stephen Roe, Duncan Woodburn
Structural engineers: Ove Arup & Partners (Dublin)
Services engineers: Building Design Partnership (Dublin)
Main contractor: Michael McNamara Co
Light sculpture artist: Lindsay Bloxam
Quantity surveyor: Patterson Kempter & Shortall
Total area: 5,800m^2 (3,500m^2 of new building, 2,300m^2 existing)
Cost: IR£8,000,000
Design to completion time: Planning approval August 1995, completion of work June 1997 (new building) and July 1998 (refurbishment of existing building)

Allies and Morrison

Student Union, University of Southampton, England
Type of commission: direct
Project team: Paul Appleton, Pauline Stockmans, Hattau Arabau, Kevin Allsop, Henor Thomson
Structural engineers: L G Monchel & Partners Ltd
Mechanical/electrical engineers: Andrew Wilks Management
Acoustic engineers: Robert Jackson Associates
Contractor: Ospray Integrated Projects Ltd
Schedule of main areas: Ground floor union shop, 280m^2; shop store, 36m^2; unloading area, 28m^2; first floor roof-lit gallery, 55m^2; insurance unit, 85m^2; travel agent, 75m^2; pharmacy, 75m^2; general office, 20m^2; manager's office, 10m^2; WCs, 6m^2; kitchen/rest area, 6m^2
Total area: 795m^2
Cost: £420,000

Design to completion time: Begun summer 1994, completed July 1995

Patrick Berger & Jacques Anziutti

Maison de l'Université de Bourgogne, Dijon, France
Type of commission: competition
Project team: Patrick Berger, Jacques Anziutti (architects); Janine Galiano, Marc Bigarnet (assistants)
Structural engineers: Batiserf
Economist: Y Guiheneuf
Fluid engineer: L Choulet
Landscape architect: Franck Neau
Total area: 6,300m^2
Cost: FF37,000,000
Design to completion time: 1992 to 1996

De Blacam & Meagher

The Atrium and Dining Hall, Trinity College, Dublin, Ireland
Project team: Shane De Blacam, John Meagher, Martin Donnelly
Structural engineers: Lee McCullough & Partners
Mechanical/electrical engineers: Homan O'Brien Associates
Contractor: Crampton Ltd (Dublin)
Lighting consultant: John Bridgefield
Total area: 5,000m^2 approx
Cost: £5,000,000
Design to completion time: 1984 to 1986

De Blacam & Meagher

Cork Institute of Technology Library, Cork, Ireland
Project team: Shane De Blacam, John Meagher, Mary Laheen, Lawrence Fewer
Structural engineers: Horgan, Lynch & Partners
Mechanical/electrical engineers: Martin Buckley & Associates
Contractor: Rohcon Ltd
Quantity surveyor: Patrick Coveney Partnership
Total area: 5,000m^2 approx
Cost: £5,000,000
Design to completion time: 1991 to 1996

De Blacam & Meagher
School of Art, Cluain Mhuire, Galway, Ireland
Type of commission: competition
Project team: Shane De Blacam, Pierre Long, Neil Crimmins
Structural engineers: Lee McCullough & Partners
Mechanical/electrical engineers: Varming Mulcahy Reilly Associates
Contractor: Michael Fitzgerald & Sons Ltd
Schedule of main areas: Sculpture workshop, 500m² library, 154m² existing building, 3,000m²
Total area: 3,654m²
Cost: £2,300,000
Design to completion time: 1998 to 1999

Odile Decq Benoit Cornette Associates
School of Economic Sciences and Law Library, University of Nantes, France
Type of commission: competition
Structural engineers: Terrell International
Mechanical engineers: S GE Co
Electrical engineers: CIEC
Acoustic engineers: Peutz & Associates
Landscape consultant: Bruel-Delmar
Schedule of main areas: Library, 4,000m²; Faculty of Economic Sciences, 8,000m²
Total area: 12,000m²
Cost: FF45,000,000
Design to completion time: 1994 to 1998

Jeremy Dixon, Edward Jones Architects
Croydon University Campus Masterplan, Croydon, England
Project team: Jeremy Dixon, Edward Jones, Mark Bunting
Design date: 1993

Jeremy Dixon, Edward Jones Architects Darwin College Study Centre, University of Cambridge, England
Type of commission: limited competition
Project team: Jeremy Dixon, Edward Jones, Pascal Madoc-Jones, John Parker, John Moran, Wal Chuen Chan
Structural/mechanical/electrical engineers: Ove Arup & Partners
Acoustic engineers: Arup Acoustics
Contractor: Rattee and Kett
Other consultants: Davis Langdon & Everest
Landscape architect: Janet Jack
Total area: 1,000m²
Cost: £1,000,000
Design to completion time: June 1989 to March 1994

Jeremy Dixon, Edward Jones Architects Science Building, University of Portsmouth, England
Type of commission: competition
Project team: Jeremy Dixon, Edward Jones, Mark Bunting, Gordon Cousins, Louise Cotter, Pascal Madoc-Jones, John Moran, David Naessens, John Parker
Structural/mechanical/electrical engineers: Rust Consulting
Acoustic engineers: Alan Saunders Associates
Civil engineers:
Contractor: Wimpey Construction SE
Quantity surveyor: Gleeds
Other consultants: Department of Education
Total area: 6,500m²
Cost: £8,250,000
Design to completion time: July 1992 to March 1996

Sir Norman Foster & Partners: Lycée Albert Camus, Fréjus, France
Type of commission: competition
Project team: Norman Foster, Sabiha Foster, Spencer de Grey, Ken Shuttleworth, John Silver, Mouzhan Majidi, Max Neal, Simon Bowden, Glenis Fan, Jason Flanagan, Michael Jones, Kate Peake, Giles Robinson, Cindy Walters, Ken Wai (London); Alex Reid, Tim Quick Bronagh Carey, Eric Jappres, Kriti Siderakis (France)
Structural engineers: Ove Arup & Partners
Services engineers: J Roger Preston
Acoustic engineers: Sandy Brown Associates
Contractors: Sobatra / Nord France (building); Sogev (external)
Lighting consultant: Claude Engle Lighting Consultants
Quantity surveyors: Davis Langdon & Everest
Specifications: Thorne Wheatley Associates
Landscape architect: Desvigne & Dalnoky
Total area: 14,500m²
Cost: FF80,000,000
Design to completion time: June 1991 to August 1993

Sir Norman Foster & Partners
Faculty of Management Robert Gordon University, Aberdeen, Scotland
Type of commission: invited interview
Project team: Norman Foster, Ken Shuttleworth, Nigel Dancey, Lulie Fisher, Andy Purvis, John Small, Toby Blunt, Mark Atkinson, Chris Bubb, Steve Best Geoff Bee, Egon Hansen, Gordon Seles, Paul Simms, Mike Oades
Structural engineers: Ove Arup & Partners
Mechanical/electrical engineers: Hully and Kirkwood

Acoustic engineers: Sandy Brown Associates
Contractor: Bovis Construction Ltd
Specification writer: Schumann Smith
Fire consultants: Dr Eric Marchant, Edinburgh Fire Consultants Ltd
Landscape architect: Ian White Associates
Total area: 12,500m^2
Cost: £13,750,000 approx
Design to completion time: 1994 to 1997

Sir Norman Foster & Partners

Faculty of Law, University of Cambridge, England
Type of commission: competition
Project team: Norman Foster, Spencer de Grey, John Silver, Chris Connell, Michael Jones, Mouzhan Majidi, Guiseppe Boscherini, Angus Campbell, Glenis Fan, Jason Flanagan, Lucy Highton, Ben Marshall, Divya Patel, Kate Peake, Victoria Pike, Austin Relton, Giles Robinson, John Small, Ken Wai, Cindy Walters, Ricarda Zimmerer
Structural engineers: Anthony Hunt Associates
Services engineers: YRM Engineers
Acoustic engineers: Sandy Brown Associates
Contractor: Taylor Woodrow Construction Southern Ltd
Lighting consultant: ERCO Ltd
Quantity surveyors: Davis Langdon & Everest
Cladding consultant: Emmer Pfenniger Partner AG
Fire engineering: Ove Arup & Partners
Pedestrian consultant: Halcrow Fox
Landscape architect: Cambridge Landscape Architects
Total area: 9,000m^2
Cost: £12,400,000
Design to completion time: 1990 to 1995

Henri Gaudin

Extension of Faculty of Sciences, Université Saint-Leu, Amiens, France
Type of commission: competition
Engineers: OTH Bâtiments
Contractor: Ville d'Amiens
Total area: 7,800m^2
Cost: FHT64,000,000
Design to completion time: July 1990 to March 1993

Grafton Architects

Department of Mechanical Engineering, Parsons Building, Trinity College, Dublin, Ireland
Type of commission: appointment by interview
Project team: Shelley McNamara, Yvonne Farrell, Eilis O'Donnell, Alastair Hall, Gerard Carty, Philippe O'Sullivan (models & collage)
Structural engineers: Ove Arup & Partners
Mechanical/electrical engineers: Homan O'Brien Associates
Contractor: John Paul Construction
Quantity surveyors: Patterson Kempter & Shortall
Glazing consultant: Sean Billings
Schedule of main areas: Workshop and laboratories, 550m^2; acoustics laboratory, 100m^2; two seminar rooms, 168m^2 postgraduate studies, 84m^2; offices and ancillary spaces, 196m^2
Total area: 1,100m^2
Cost: IR£1,100,000
Design to completion time: 1994 to 1996

Hampshire County Architects / Perkins Ogden Architects

Hackney Community College, London, England
Type of commission: competition
Project team: Steve Clow (HCA), Garry Vanscreech (HCA), Mervyn Perkins (POA), Nick Collett (POA), Anthony Munden (POA), Gareth Williams (POA) & Bird
Structural/mechanical/electrical engineers: Whitby & Bird (Bath/London), Buro Happold (London)
Acoustic engineers: Arup Acoustics (Winchester)
Contractors: Carillion Building (formerly Talmac Construction), John Sisk & Son, Kier London, Mullaley Contractors
Lighting consultant: Whitby & Bird (London), Buro Happold
Landscape architect: Pearson Landscapes
Total area: Phase 1 (main campus teaching, learning resources and science), 20,000m^2; phase 2 (sports, recreation and dance centre), 2,700m^2; phase 3 (multimedia centre), 3,600m^2
Cost: £40,000,000
Design to completion time: Summer 1993 to summer 2000

Hampshire County Architects

Portland Street Building, University of Portsmouth, England
Type of commission: direct
Project team: Sir Colin Stansfield-Smith, Alec Upton, Bob Wallbridge, Tina Bird, Fred Chaney, Mike Keys, Adrian Curtis
Structural engineers: Buro Happold, Bath
Mechanical/electrical engineers: Hampshire County Architects
Project managers: Bovis Program Management, Harrow
Contractor: Norwest Holt Construction Ltd

Total area: 6228m^2
Cost: £5,854,320
Design to completion time: February 1993 to August 1995

Hodder Associates

Career Services Unit, University of Manchester, England
Type of commission: competition
Project team: Stephen Hodder, Jolyon Brewis, Theo Bishop, Robert Evans, Martin Gibson, Victoria Hilton, Rud Sawers
Structural engineers: Blackwood Structural Design
Mechanical/electrical engineers: Miller Walmsley Partnership
Contractor: W. Snape & Sons
Total area: 1162.75m^2
Cost: £1,340,000
Design to completion time: September 1994 to December 1995

Hodder Associates

Centenary Building, University of Salford, England
Type of commission: direct
Project team: Stephen Hodder, Richard Blackwell, Robert Evans, Neil Clarke, Vetus Lau, Christian Male
Structural engineers: SMP Atelier One
Mechanical/electrical engineers: Miller Walmsley Partnership
Contractor: AMEC Design & Management
Total area: 3623m^2
Cost: £3,200,000
Design to completion time: November 1996 to February 1998

Michael Hopkins and Partners

Jubilee Campus, University of Nottingham, England
Type of commission: competition
Project team: Sir Michael Hopkins, William Taylor, Bill Dunster, Simon Fraser, Jan Mackie, Matthew Hoad, Uli Moeller, Toki Hochirio, Rachel Sayers, Eric Sverikerud
Structural/mechanical/electrical engineers: Ove Arup & Partners
Acoustic engineers: Arup Acoustics
Contractor: Bovis Construction Ltd
Landscape architect: Battle McCarthy
Project manager: Mace Ltd.
Schedule of main areas: School of Management & Finance, 4,300m^2; Department of Computer Science, Faculty of Education and central catering facility, 13,600m^2; central teaching facility, 4,000m^2; learning resource centre, 1,800m^2; postgraduate halls, 3,500m^2; undergraduate halls, 13,300m^2
Total area: 40,500m^2
Cost: £37,000,000

Michael Hopkins and Partners

The Queen's Building, Emmanuel College, University of Cambridge, England
Project team: Sir Michael Hopkins, Lady Hopkins, James Greaves, Michael Taylor, Mark Turkel, Buddy Haward
Structural/mechanical/electrical engineers: Buro Happold
Acoustic engineers: Arup Acoustics
Contractor: Sir Robert McAlpine Management Contracting Ltd
Lighting consultant: John Marsteller / George Sexton
Total area: 1,200m^2
Cost: £4,300,000

Mecanoo

Faculty of Economics and Management, Utrecht Polytechnic, The Netherlands
Project team: Francine Houben, Erick van Egeraat, Chris de Wijer, Henk Döll, Monica Adams, Aart Fransen, Marjolijn Adriaansche, Carlo Bevers, Gerrit Bras, Giuseppina Borri, Birgit de Bruin, Henk Bouwer, Ard Buijsen, Katja van Dalen, Annemiek Diekman, Harry Kurzhals, Miranda Nieboer, William Richards, Mechtild Stuhlmacher, Nathalie de Vries, Wim van Zijl
Structural engineers: ABT adviesbureau voor bouwtechniek b.v., Delft/Velp
Mechanical/electrical engineers: Technical Management b.v., Amersfoort
Contractor: Hollandse Beton Maatshappij b.v., Utrecht
Management consultants: PRC Management Consultants b.v., Bodegraven
Artists: Gera van der Leun, Henk Metselaar, Linda Verkaaik
Total area: 23,500m^2 approx
Cost: DFl 40,000,000
Design to completion time: Design 1991 to 1992; construction September 1993 to May 1995

Neutelings Riedijk

Minnaert Building, University of Utrecht, The Netherlands
Project team: Willem Jan Neutelings, Michiel Riedijk, Jonathan Woodroffe, Evert Crols, Jago van Bergen, Gerrit Schilder, Burton Hamfelt, Chidi Onquka, Joost Mulders
Structural design: ABT Adviesbureau voor bouwtechniek b.v., Velp
Building services engineering: Ingenieursburo Linssen b.v., Amsterdam
Contractor: Aanneming Maatschappij J.P. van Eesteren b.v., Rotterdam
Building physics consultant: Adviesbureau Peutz & Associes b.v., Molenhoek
Interior architects: N.R.A and F.B.U. (Facility Management University)

Landscape architects: West 8 Landscape Architects b.v., Rotterdam
Artists: Frans Parthesius, Perry Roberts, Tejo Remy
Total area: 9,000m² approx
Design to completion time: 1994–1997

John Outram
Duncan Hall, William Marsh Rice University, Texas
Type of commission: appointment by interview
Design architects: John Outram Associates
Executive architects: Kendall Heaton Associates
Structural engineering consultants: Walter P. Moore and Associates, Inc.
Mechanical/electrical engineers: I. A. Naman + Associates, Inc.
Managing contractor: Lott Construction with Brown & Root
Lighting consultant: Richard Jeter
Cost consultant: Gardiner & Theobald
Landscape design consultants: Sasaki Associates
Total area: 120,000 sq ft
Cost: $16,500,000
Design to completion time: June 1993 to August 1996

John Outram
Judge Institute of Management Studies, University of Cambridge, England
Type of commission: competition
Project team: David Bass, Natasha Black, Anthony Charnley, Wendy Dellit, Iona Foster, Felna Fox, Rebecca Granger, Elizabeth Gregory, Bill Gregory, Timothy Hall, Raida Kassim Bench, Sally MacKay, Glen Millar, Jean Murphy, Nina Noor, John Outram, Huw Owen, Amir Ramezani, Jeremiah Sheehan, Alan Smith-Oliver
Structural engineering consultants: Felix Samuely Partnership
Mechanical/electrical engineers: Max Fordham & Partners
Contractor: Laing (Eastern) Ltd.
Cost consultants: Davis Langdon and Everest (Cambridge)
Landscape design consultants: Holden and Liversedge
Total area: 9,000m²
Cost: £11,000,000
Design to completion time: April 1991 to September 1995

Eric Parry Architects
Sussex Innovation Centre, Falmer, Brighton, England
Type of commission: competition
Project team: Eric Parry, Philip Meadowcroft, Robert Kennett (project architect), Nello Gregori, Nick Jackson
Structural/mechanical/electrical engineers: Ove Arup & Partners

Contractor: Wates
Landscape architects: East Sussex County Council Planning Department
Schedule of main areas: Café, 90m²; conference room, 50m²; administrative areas, 90m²; tenant office/semilaboratory, 1,400m²
Total area: 1860m²
Cost: £1,650,000 (excluding fit out)
Design to completion time: August 1994 to May 1996

Antoine Predock Architect
Student Affairs & Administrative Services Building, University of California Santa Barbara, California
Type of commission: direct
Project team: Antoine Predock (principal-in-charge), Douglas Friend (associate-in-charge), Lawrence Mead (project manager), Geoffrey Bee, W Anthony Evanko, Mark Donahue, Paul Gonzales, Cathy Hahn, Robert McElheney, George Newlands, Kira Sowanick, Deborah Waldrip, Luke Bulman, Aron Idoine, Curtis Scharfenaker
Structural engineers: Paragon Structural Design, Inc.
Mechanical/electrical engineers: JBA Consulting Engineers
Civil engineers: RBA Partners
Contractor: McCormick Construction
Total area: 75,000 sq ft
Cost: $11,817,000
Design to completion time: 1992 to 1997

Antoine Predock Architect
Faculty of Music, University of California Santa Cruz, California
Type of commission: direct
Project team: Antoine Predock (principal-in-charge), Devendra Contractor (project architect), Geoffrey Adams, Jon Anderson, Sunil Bald, Jorge Burbano, Phyllis Cece, Mark Donahue, Cameron Erdmann, Mischa Farrell, Lorraine Guthrie, Katherine Howe, Karen King, Robert McElheney, George Newlands, Timothy Nichols, Brett Oaks, Christopher Romero, Alcides Santiesteban, Deborah Waldrip, Suzanne Weisman, Jeffrey Wren
Structural engineers: Paragon Structural Design, Inc.
Mechanical/electrical engineers: JBA Consulting Engineers
Acoustic engineers: McKay Conant Brook, Inc.
Civil engineers: Chavez-Grievex
Contractor: Lewis C Nelson & Sons
Landscape architects: Jon L Janecki & Associates
Schedule of main areas:
Total area: 38,000 sq ft
Cost: $12,000,000
Design to completion time: 1990 to 1996

Richard Rogers Partnership
Paul Hamlyn Learning Resource Centre, Thames Valley
University, Slough, England
Type of commission: direct
Project team: Maurice Brennan, Mark Darbon, Michael Davies,
Chris Donnington, Michael Elkan, Michael Fairbrass, Marco
Goldschmied, Philip Gumuchdjian, Jackie Hands, Avery Howe,
Sharni Howe, Amarjit Kalsi, Carol Painter, Louise Palomba,
Richard Rogers, Stephen Spence, John Young
Structural/services/mechanical/electrical engineers: Buro
Happold
Contractor: Laing South East
Lighting consultant: Lighting Design Partnership
Quantity surveyor: Hanscomb
Sculptor: Danny Lane
Landscape architect: Edward Hutchison
Total area: 3,500m^2
Cost: £3,600,000
Design to completion time: May 1994 to April 1996

Short & Associates (formerly Short, Ford & Associates)
Queen's Building, De Montfort University, Leicester, England
Project team: Alan Short, Brian Ford, Anne Goldrick, Peter
Sharrat
Structural/civil engineers: YRM Anthony Hunt Associates
**Mechanical/electrical/acoustic engineers & lighting con-
sultants:** Max Fordham & Partners
Contractor: Laing
Other consultants: Institute of Energy and sustainability, De
Montfort University; Department of Applied Mathematics and
Theoretical Physics, Cambridge University
Landscape architect: Georgina Livinstone-Eyre
Schedule of main areas:
Total area: 10,000m^2
Cost: £8,700,000
Completed: September 1993

Souto Moura Arquitectos Lda
Department of Geosciences, Aveiro University, Portugal
Project team: David Adjaye, Marie Clement, Graça Correia,
Joaquim Dias da Silva, José Fernando Gonçalves, Teresa
Gonçalves, Manuela Lara, Pedro Mendes, João Nuno Pereira,
Adriana Pimenta, Filipe Pinto da Cruz, Pedro Reis, Eduardo
Souto de Moura, Francisco Vieira de Campos, Anne Wermeille
Structural/mechanical/electrical engineers: Encil
Contractor: Cobetar
Total area: 4,314m^2
Design to completion time: 1989 to 1994

James Stirling Michael Wilford and Associates
Temasek Polytechnic, Singapore
Project team: James Stirling Michael Wilford and Associates;
DP Architects Pts, Singapore (associate architects)
Structural engineers: Ove Arup, Singapore
Mechanical/electrical engineers: Ewbank Preece Engineers
Plc, Singapore
Acoustic engineers: Arup Acoustics, London; Acviron, Singapore
Structural, mechanical, electrical and special services: Ove
Arup & Partners
Project management: Public Works Department, Singapore
Quantity surveyors: KPK, Singapore
Landscape architect: PDAA, Singapore
Schedule of main areas: Administration, music school and
library, 33,750m^2; large auditorium (600 seats), 700m^2; multi-
purpose auditorium (250 seats), 300m^2; School of Applied
Science, 36,260m^2; School of Technology, 70,850m^2; School of
Business, 20,110m^2; School of Design, 14,869m^2; student
centre and central canteen, 5,800m^2; faculty club and
childcare, 2,480m^2; multipurpose sports hall, 6,680m^2; swim-
ming complex, 1,640m^2; staff housing (102 apartments),
22,570m^2
Total area: 215,000m^2
Cost: S$380,000,000 (£165,000,000)
Design to completion time: 1991 to 1995

Michael Wilford & Partners
Music Academy, Stuttgart, Germany
Structural engineers: Ove Arup & Partners, London; Boll &
Partner, Stuttgart
Mechanical services/public health engineers: Ove Arup &
Partners, London/Stuttgart; Jaeger Mornhinweg & Partner,
Stuttgart
Electrical engineers: Ove Arup & Partners, London; Inge-
nieurbüo, Stuttgart
Acoustic engineers: Arup Acoustics, London; Müller BBM,
Munich
Building physics: Dr Flohrer, Berlin
Contractor: Wolff + Müller GmbH, Stuttgart
Kitchen planners: Becker, Stuttgart
Cost consultants: Davis Langdon and Everest, London
Site supervision: Michael Weiss, Aachen
Schedule of main areas: Concert hall, 660m^2; library, 250m^2;
studios, rehearsal rooms and classrooms, 600m^2; dining room,
5,000m^2; administrative offices, 220m^2; foyers, circulation,
support and ancillary spaces, 460m^2
Total area: 20,830m^2
Cost: DM90,000,000
Design to completion time: 1986 to 1996

SELECT BIBLIOGRAPHY

C Alexander, *The city is not a tree (part 2)*, Architectural Forum, May 1965.

W H G Armytage, *Civic Universities*, Benn (London), 1955.

M Brawne, *University of Virginia; the lawn; Thomas Jefferson*, Phaidon Press 1994.

M Brawne (ed), *University planning and design, a symposium*. Published for the Architectural Association by Lund Humphries, 1967.

L Brett, *Architectural Review*, October 1963.

Sir Sydney Caine, *British Universities*, Bodley Head (London), 1969.

Alan B Cobban, *The Medieval Universities*, Methuen (London), 1975.

R Dober, 1996, *Campus Architecture*, Reinhold (New York), 1963.

H H Green, *A History of Oxford University*, Batsford, (London), 1974.

S W A Hawking, *A Brief History of Time; from big bang to black holes*, Bantam Press (London), 1988.

W Mitchell, *City of Bits; Space Place and the Infobahn*, MIT Press, 1995.

J H Newman, *The Idea of a University*, Yale University Press (New Haven), 1996.

Royal Fine Arts Commission, *Design Quality in Higher Education*, Telford (London), 1996.

Royal Fine Arts Commission, *Design Quality in Higher Education*, Telford (London), 1996.

J Rykwert, 'Universities as institutional archetypes of our age', *Zodiac 18*

D Smith and A K Langslow (eds), *The Idea of a University*, Jessica Kingsley, (London), 1999.

Bruce Truscot, *Red Brick Universities*, Pelican Books (Harmondsworth).